RESTLESS IN THE PROMISED LAND

THIIS SIDE OF PARADISE

Scott and Zelda Fitzgerald on their honeymoon, 1920. He was Catholic and she was Episcopalian, but religion didn't seem to matter much in the heady years following their marriage, when the couple seemed to embody the American Dream of fast cars, big houses, and effortless fame in all its shimmering possibility. Yet Scott's Catholic heritage cast shadows—and deepened his art, most notably *The Great Gatsby*—in ways that would have lasting consequences even after both of their lives had been battered by illness, defeat, and rejection. *(Photo from the Collections of the Library of Congress)*

RESTLESS IN THE PROMISED LAND

Catholics and the American Dream

*Portraits of a spiritual quest
from the time of the Puritans to the present*

JIM CULLEN

SHEED & WARD
FRANKLIN, WISCONSIN

As an apostolate of the Priests of the Sacred Heart, a Catholic religious congregation, the mission of Sheed & Ward is to publish books of contemporary impact and enduring merit in Catholic Christian thought and action. The books published, however, reflect the opinions of their authors and are not meant to represent the official position of the Priests of the Sacred Heart.

Sheed & Ward
7373 South Lovers Lane Road
Franklin, Wisconsin 53132
1800–266–5564

Cover and interior design by Madonna Gauding
Cover photos, from left to right: Willem Dafoe and Martin Scorsese: Photo courtesy of the Kobal Collection, New York; Margaret Mitchell: Photo by William Warnecke from the New York World-Telegram & Sun Collection, Library of Congress; Madonna: Photo by Herb Ritts courtesy of the Kobal Collection, New York; F. Scott Fitzgerald: Photo from the Collections of the Library of Congress.

Library of Congress Cataloging–in–Publication Data

Cullen, Jim, 1962–
    Restless in the promised land : Catholics and the American dream : Portraits of a spiritual quest from the time of the Puritans to the present / Jim Cullen.
   p. cm.
    Includes bibliographical references (p.).
    ISBN 1-58051-093-0
        1.   Catholic Church—United States—History. 2. United States—Church history. I. Title.

BX1406.2 .C78 2001
305.6'2073—dc21

       2001020136

1 2 3 4 * 04 03 02 01

Printed in the United States of America

OTHER BOOKS BY JIM CULLEN

The Civil War in Popular Culture:
A Reusable Past

The Art of Democracy:
A Concise History of Popular Culture in the United States

Born in the U.S.A.:
Bruce Springsteen and the American Tradition

Popular Culture in American History (editor)

For my aunt,
Helen Montani,
and the gift of her faith

CONTENTS

ACKNOWLEDGMENTS *xi*

Introduction
THE SOULS OF CATHOLIC FOLK *xv*

PART I
DEFINING THE DREAM *1*

    Chapter One
    THE COMPLEXITIES OF THE AMERICAN DREAM *3*

    Chapter Two
    THE ANTI-CATHOLIC ORIGINS OF THE AMERICAN DREAM *17*

PART II
EMBODYING THE DREAM: AMERICAN CATHOLIC ARCHETYPES *43*

    Chapter Three
    FATAL ATTRACTION: THE CASE OF JAY GATSBY *45*

    Chapter Four
    INCOMPLETE DENIAL: THE CASE OF SCARLETT O'HARA *65*

    Chapter Five
    LIKE A HERETIC: THE CASE OF MADONNA *85*

    Chapter Six
    IT'S A WONDERFUL DEATH:
    THE CASE OF (MARTIN SCORSESE'S) JESUS CHRIST *109*

    Conclusion
    THE SOULS OF KINGS *137*

ENDNOTES *143*

SOURCES AND NOTES *145*

INDEX *159*

ACKNOWLEDGMENTS

This book exists because of June Sawyers. In the summer of 1997 June read my book *Born in the U.S.A.*, and was particularly interested in my chapter on the Catholic dimension of Bruce Springsteen's music. She thought I might be able to write an entire book on Catholicism and popular culture, and wrote me a letter suggesting I do so. I wasn't sure I could. For one thing, I was tied up with other projects. For another, I didn't know if I had enough to say in an entire book. But June, who at any given point seems to be juggling a half-dozen writing projects of her own, raised the subject again via email in the fall of 1999. It so happened that another book project I was working on about the American Dream had been put on hold. I suddenly saw that I had the opportunity to write a book on Catholicism, and the American Dream might just be the peg I could hang it on.

This would have been as far as the book went had not Jeremy Langford, the youthful editor–in–chief of the venerable Sheed & Ward, gotten involved. Jeremy's enthusiasm for the project was infectious, and I will always be grateful for his encouragement.

I also need to put in a word of thanks to Jeremy's father, Jim Langford, formerly of the University of Notre Dame Press and now with Rowman and Littlefield. Incredibly, he picked up the manuscript while in the hospital recuperating from bypass surgery, and read it carefully enough to pass on invaluable advice to me through his son. While I imagine his family might plausibly scold him for what seems like an irrepressible work ethic, I'm grateful to benefit from his curiosity and insight (not to mention his recovery).

In more official capacities, I am grateful for the goodwill and professionalism of Kass Dotterweich, who shepherded the manuscript into print, and the artistry of designer Madonna Gauding.

ACKNOWLEDGMENTS

In order to write this book, I was forced to stray from my usual disciplinary pen of secular American cultural history, and did not have the benefit of a pool of like-minded colleagues whose wisdom I could easily draw upon. I was thus especially glad for the friendship of my childhood friend Robert Falvo, professor of music at Appalachian State University, whose own foray into Zen Buddhism was a useful foil for mine into our shared Catholic heritage, and Ron Afzal, professor of religion at Sarah Lawrence College, whose off-hand remark about the latent Catholicism of Joan Osborne's 1995 song "One of Us"—with its comic image of the pope having a hotline to heaven—emboldened me to think I might really be able to write a book about such things. (The blame for actually doing so, of course, is mine alone.)

   A number of people are responsible for the fact I could write it. My boss, Nancy Sommers of the Expository Writing Program at Harvard University, has for some years now tolerated a writing instructor who has taken leaves to write books and raise children. Two friends, Heather Winn and Lara Haggar, were around for my three sons when I was not, and gave me the gift of time many times when I was. I can't quite claim those three sons made it easy to write the book. But I can thank them for the pleasure of their company (diaper changes not included).

   My parents, Grace and Jim Cullen, gave me the spiritual foundation I have tried to build on here and elsewhere, and even now their quiet faith gives me courage. My sister Cathy has practiced her own faith in ways that remain an example for me. And my in–laws, Ted and Nancy Sizer, have been role models—and sources of support—that grow ever more humbling as I grow older.

   A final word of thanks to my wife, Lyde Cullen Sizer. An heir of the Puritans, she embodies the very best of what they represented— and her tolerance of me single-handedly proves she has escaped their worst vices. It's a mystery how she does it. But boy, am I glad she does.

Jim Cullen
Bronxville, New York
April 2001

SOUL MAN

W. E. B. DuBois (1868–1963) photographed by the famed documen-
tarian Carl Van Vechten in 1948. By the end of his life, DuBois, repeatedly
harassed by the American government for his political views, was em-
bittered by what he regarded as the cruelly false promises of the American
Dream. But the sense of "double consciousness" he spoke of in his most
famous book, *The Soul of Black Folk,* remains a singularly illuminating
lens through which all Americans—black or not, religious or not, disillusioned or not—might better understand their place in
their society. *(Photo from the Van Vechten Collection of the Library of
Congress)*

Introduction

THE SOULS OF CATHOLIC FOLK

In his 1903 book *The Souls of Black Folk*, the famed African-American scholar W. E. B. DuBois described his fellow descendants of slaves as "gifted with second–sight in this American world." He went on to explain what he meant by this in one of the most celebrated passages in twentieth–century American history:

> It is a peculiar sensation, this double–consciousness, this sense of always looking at oneself through the eyes of others, of measuring one's soul by the tape of a world that looks on in amused contempt and pity. One ever feels his two-ness—an American, a Negro; two souls, two thoughts, two unreconciled strivings; two warring ideals in one dark body, whose dogged strength alone keeps it from being torn asunder.

"The history of the American Negro is the history of this strife," he asserted.

The lasting fame of *The Souls of Black Folk* testifies to the clarity of DuBois's vision. But what seems almost as striking is the degree to which his words, singularly applicable as they are for African Americans specifically, also go to the heart of the American experience generally. For there have in fact been many people in our history who have experienced a kind of double consciousness—and have been recipients of "contempt and pity": Indians, Asians, Latinos. So have immigrants from Europe and their children. Race, class, ethnicity, and gender are among the many reasons why some people have had an uneasy relationship with the land that became the United States.

Always important, even primary, among those reasons has been religion. American Jews are one obvious example of people who have experienced ambivalence and exclusion in a place they and gentiles alike have called "the promised land." So too have many varieties of Protestants, among them Quakers, Mennonites, and Mormons. Even the Puritans who helped found this nation (about whom I'll have a good deal to say in the pages that follow) often described themselves as caught between worlds—old and new, sacred and secular.

Roman Catholics fit squarely into this model of American history. Indeed, in the nineteenth century in particular, when waves of Irish and other immigrants began to arrive in growing numbers, there are few people *other* than African Americans for whom DuBois's words would be more apt. Like African Americans, white Catholics strived to gain a place in American life even as they tried to preserve their heritage amid much resistance. There are, of course, significant differences, even ironies, in African–American and Catholic–American histories. One difference—given the significant amount of attention, mostly negative, both received for centuries—is the relatively small degree of integration in their experiences (notwithstanding important exceptions like Georgetown University founder Patrick Healy and long-standing black communities along the Gulf of Mexico). Another is the regrettable degree to which Catholics, who were subject to all kinds of discrimination themselves, nevertheless contributed to, and benefited from, racism, whether in their displacement as targets of hatred as African Americans moved North in the great migrations of the twentieth century, or in actually exploiting black labor themselves. A third is the relative speed with which Catholics, who were generally much later arrivals, were permitted by ruling white Protestant elites to enter the mainstream of American life more quickly.

In many respects, the last century witnessed a struggle for *all* Americans, whatever their identities, to put the "contempt and pity" DuBois wrote about behind them. Without suggesting such problems are wholly a thing of the past—Catholics, who tend to be skeptical about the complete success of any worldly reform, typically doubt they'll *ever* be—there has nevertheless been significant improvement. And yet, whether by choice, heritage, or the wiles of psychology, a sense of double consciousness remains widespread in American life.

This is particularly true of American Catholics. Notwithstanding the significant number of people who convert as adults, Catholicism is typically an inherited identity, and not one—as countless examples attest—that even the most committed apostate can easily shake. Catholics become Americans; Catholics even embrace other religions; and yet the "mother church," as it is sometimes called, lays claim to allegiances that are somehow never wholly a matter of choice.

To be an American, by contrast, is usually viewed as a matter of choice. In part, this is because millions of people are, or are recently descended from, people who left their place of origin to pledge their allegiance to this country. But there's more to it than that. Even for those whose heritage stretches back many generations, American identity is premised on an ever-renewable future. Whatever our manifold differences, virtually all of us pledge allegiance to a highly malleable pursuit of happiness that has come to be known as "the American Dream."

This book is about that ideal, and its often perplexing relationship to Catholicism.

Before delving into any detail, I thought it would be worthwhile to describe the standpoint from which I write it. My own experience—my own double consciousness—is both deeply personal and widely shared. It has some specific contours, and it is probably useful to be as explicit as I can to suggest the ways in which my perspective is different, as well as similar, to that of other American Catholics (and non–Catholics).

Perhaps the first thing I should say is that like many Catholics, my relationship with the Church has been fitful. As I child I was deeply moved and engaged by biblical stories and, as a child of an Irish father and an Italian mother, I saw the Church as central in my family's cultural and social life: a recurrent cycle of Christmas and Easter gifts, celebrations of communions and confirmations, and catechism classes at a local Catholic school each week. Coming of age in the aftermath of Vatican II—to this day I have never heard a mass in Latin—my churchgoing was at times a steady ritual, but often an empty one, characterized by enervating sermons, a wandering attention span, and close tracking of the clock mounted over the rear doors of the church. Adolescence and early adulthood brought with it a conscious rejection of much church doctrine and an often inchoate search for a more intellectually compatible religious framework. On those occasions when I attended the campus chapel in my undergraduate years, it was for non–denominational Protestant services.

I was far less ambivalent about my identity as an American, and immersed myself in learning about this country—from histories of the American Revolution to the current hits on the pop charts—from an early age. (Church music seemed almost illegitimate to me, an idiom wholly apart from, and thus not really relevant to, the world in which I was living.) An eager student, I went on to earn a Ph.D. in American Civilization, and wrote a series of books about the history of popular culture.

It was one of those books, a study of Bruce Springsteen's music and its place in American cultural history, that began to turn my attention back toward religion generally and Catholicism specifically. Studying Springsteen's work, it was impossible to ignore the way his own Catholic upbringing had decisively shaped his music, both in ways that seemed entirely conscious (usually a matter of thumbing his nose at it) as well as instinctive and perhaps unwitting. I included a chapter on Springsteen's religious vision in the book, alongside others on topics such as gender, the Vietnam War, and his even more obvious obsession with the American Dream.

Perhaps not surprisingly, the American Dream is also an obsession of mine, and my work in recent years has focused on tracing its history. This book, a branch of that larger effort, grew out from my recognition of the fundamentally religious foundations of the American Dream, foundations that I, along with many others, have often overlooked. It also grew out of a recognition that some of the most provocative commentary on the Dream in American culture came from people who, like me, happened to be Catholics. Increasingly, I've found, the part of myself that I've tended to view as somehow apart from my interests has become crucial in trying to make sense of them. And so it was that I began to compose the words which you are now reading.

The process of writing the book has led me to realize just how shallowly I'm digging below the surface in uncovering the relationship between Catholicism and the American Dream. Yet even the slight depth of my inquiry has resulted in some fairly detailed explanation, and I apologize in advance for those moments (like my description of sixteenth-century Protestant theology in chapter two) that may seem a little dry, but which I regard as essential to understanding essential aspects of the Dream in contemporary American life.

That said, the book is composed of two parts. The first, "Defining the Dream," has a historical orientation. Using the present as a point of departure, chapter one, "The Complexities of the American Dream," explores some of the most common versions of the Dream and the paradox that what we commonly consider a secular idea actually has sacred origins. Chapter two, "The Anti-Catholic Origins of the American Dream," traces the roots of the Dream back to two of the most important major social revolutions of the last thousand years: the Reformation and the European colonization of the western hemisphere. The chapter focuses on a small group of Protestant dissidents who have come to be known as the Puritans. For Roman Catholics, it proved to be highly significant that the value of the Puritan American Dream was measured in its distance, literally and figuratively, from the Vatican. This reality would shape sacred as well as secular Catholic experience in America for hundreds of years, playing a major role in the formation of Catholic double consciousness.

The intellectual framework of Part II, "Embodying the Dream," takes a little more explaining, because it is based on premises that may not be immediately obvious. The first is that the Catholic relationship to the American Dream changed decisively in the twentieth century, due in large measure to the ebbing of discrimination toward Catholics and a commensurate rise of Catholic achievement and confidence in American life. Insofar as it ever makes sense to speak of *any* dream as realistic—dreams, by definition, represent aspirations that are at least a bit of a stretch—the American Dream became something with which Catholics could fully and plausibly engage. It also became something Catholics were in a position to comment on in ways that could have an impact in the culture at large.

What form has that commentary taken? Obviously, the answer is "multiple forms," ranging from the learned theological disquisition of John Courtney Murray to the discussions that animate a lively Catholic media culture that includes newspapers such as *National Catholic Reporter,* magazines such as *America* and *Commonweal,* and publishers such as the one responsible for the book you are now reading. But my focus here is different: popular culture with little or no obvious religious content, by people with little or no obvious religious commitment. In fact some of these "people" are nothing more than fictional characters, albeit characters so vivid and familiar that they might as well be real.

An odd approach, you may think. But it's one that not only represents the most accessible point of entry for someone like myself, who happens to be a historian of popular culture, but also for millions of fellow Catholics who have an intimacy with popular culture that they never have had with, say, the Nicene Creed—and who find religious meaning and content, often despite themselves, in the art of everyday life. I'm not going to claim that this content is always conscious, coherent, or finally acceptable to Church leaders, other Catholics, or Americans of other faiths (or *non*–faiths). But it is common and powerful enough to be worthy of commentary—something that Andrew Greeley, for example, has been contributing for many years. And if I lack the authority and grace of that famed sociologist, perhaps I can nevertheless serve as a specimen of the very thing I'm describing, a symptom of the problem, as it were.

These are the suppositions that guided the writing of Part II, which analyzes a few characteristic Catholic responses to the American Dream as they manifest themselves in case studies of familiar characters in our national life. (I use the word "character" here broadly, to encompass real people, invented ones, and the general notion of a defining set of traits.) Because my goal is to be brief and suggestive rather than comprehensive and irrefutable, these case studies dramatize what I regard as some of the more important responses without claiming that this exhausts the list, or that the people and works I've chosen represent the best examples. My primary reason for using them, other than my own personal interest, is that they are examples most readers are likely to have at least some familiarity with, even if they haven't read the book, seen the movie, or listened to the song in question for a while (if at all, something I don't take for granted). But the most important reason I chose these subjects is that I believe they are mirrors that reveal tendencies in American Catholicism life that remain common to this day.

The first of these case studies looks at one of the most famous characters in American literary history—Jay Gatsby, protagonist of F. Scott Fitzgerald's classic 1925 novel *The Great Gatsby*. Gatsby and Fitzgerald have long been considered archetypal figures who personify the American Dream; they're far less familiar as *Catholic* figures, for the good reason that in both cases the Catholicism of their youths was subsequently muted, even erased. And yet in important respects, both of them demonstrate a Catholic sensibility, and in one respect in particular—a sense of fatalism widely associated with Irish Catholicism—they illustrate an attitude toward American life that has been common and important for countless Americans seeking to come to terms with an elusive American Dream.

My second case study is of an even more familiar literary character, Scarlett O'Hara of *Gone with the Wind*, and her creator, Margaret Mitchell. These too are figures with powerful associations in our collective memory, particularly in regard to the Civil War. Indeed, it is no exaggeration to say that even now, the book and film versions of *Gone with the Wind* shape notions of the War Between the States in ways no history book ever has, or likely ever will. As with Gatsby/Fitzgerald, the Catholicism of O'Hara/Mitchell seems incidental, almost irrelevant. And yet a close look at these characters suggests the determination with which they sought to deny their Catholicism only made it all the more apparent how important it was in shaping them, especially with regard to the American Dream.

My third case study is of a real person, but one whose persona involves large elements of self invention: the pop star Madonna. Unlike many of the other figures I examine in the book, Madonna, whose greatest talent in the 1980s and 1990s seemed to be her skill in generating controversy, actually achieved her dream. Moreover, unlike a Jay Gatsby or a Scarlett O'Hara, Madonna was candid about her love/hate relationship with her Catholic heritage. Yet the very determination with which she embraced provocation revealed the depths of some very familiar strains of Catholic piety in her background and suggests the degree to which Madonna, who prides herself on her empowerment as a modern American woman, is still in some sense a child of the Church.

My final case study is of a man who isn't an American at all: Jesus Christ—more specifically, the Jesus Christ of Martin Scorsese's controversial 1988 film *The Last Temptation of Christ*. Though the novel on which the movie was based was written by a member of the Greek Orthodox Church and the screenplay was written by a man with a background in the Dutch Reformed Church, the film finally bears the stamp of its director, whose urban Italian Catholicism already has a mythic quality among devotees of his work. Far from the work of obscene sensationalism its critics contended it was, *The Last Temptation of Christ* is a movie of deep religious engagement. Looking carefully at how it was made can help us understand the varied strands that go into an American Catholic identity, and illustrate how works and people with *non*-American backgrounds can allow us to see works and people with unmistakably American backgrounds—such as Frank Capra's classic film *It's a Wonderful Life,* which I use as a point of comparison with *The Last Temptation of Christ*—in illuminating ways.

Though it may seem that there's a random quality in my choosing these four subjects, they do form an arc that corresponds to the trajectory of Catholic life in the twentieth century. Fitzgerald regarded his Catholicism as a problem, even an obstacle, to his literary maturation. Margaret Mitchell, by contrast, seemed to consider it irrelevant. Madonna has been willing—some might say all *too* willing—to use it in defining her public image. And Martin Scorsese, the most comfortable of the four with his heritage and the problems it poses, has self–consciously integrated it into his body of work with unusual intensity and insight. The future of Catholicism, it seems to me, will depend on the willingness of people like him and his audience to wrestle with the challenges like that posed by Charlie Cappa, the protagonist of his 1973 film *Mean Streets:* "You don't make up for your sins in Church. You do it in the streets. You do it at home. The rest is bullshit and you know it."

There is an inevitable generational dimension in the making of this book. Had I written it, say, fifty years ago, it might well have had more of an institutional and political focus (as most history,

Catholic and otherwise, did at that time). Had I written it twenty-five years ago, it might have looked a little like Jay Dolan's now classic *The American Catholic Experience,* which drew on a then-emerging social-history approach that looked at the lives of ordinary people from the ground up. Since I was trained at the end of the twentieth century as a cultural historian, or as someone who looks at the shared *ideas* of ordinary people (as opposed to their living conditions, the way a social historian would, or the ideas or lives of their leaders, as a traditional political or intellectual historian would) this book bears that stamp. That's not to say that there was no cultural history before 1990, or that there aren't plenty of other rich possibilities to write about, whether the novels of James T. Farrell, the memoirs of Mary McCarthy, or the films of John Ford. That work has, and will, be done. For better or worse, I'm just following my instincts here, and am no less a historical product than the people I write about.

Still, it's one thing to describe one's perspective; it's another to say why it matters. Is there any larger significance to what I'm saying here, other than simply tracing the way religious concerns persist among a rather unlikely group of figures? Insofar as there is any such significance, I'd say it takes the form of two different assertions. For lapsed Catholics and any non-Catholic readers I might have, I'd say that the book shows how a Catholic double consciousness can clarify both the possibilities as well as the limits of the American Dream. A richer sense of those possibilities and limits can have real consequences on the pursuit of happiness: *what* to pursue, *how* to pursue, or even *whether* to pursue particular American Dreams.

My objectives in speaking to those with an interest in the Church as an institution are a bit more complicated. Certainly, the book documents a long tradition of Catholic vitality even for those who have been "lost" by the Church. But there's more to it than that. Such people are not merely waiting to be reclaimed, or wallowing in anomie. Catholics generally and Church leaders specifically should recognize the importance of two–way communication, pay attention to the often surprising sophistication and complexity of these peoples' cultural lives, and recognize the bona fide religiosity that inheres in the Fitzgeralds, Mitchells, Madonnas, and Scorseses of our history and culture. As Catholic Americans, they are representative figures—"representative" not only in the way their issues are emblematic of others (which is why generations of Americans, Catholic and otherwise, have "voted" them into lasting prominence), but also in the way they use the artistic technique of representation—creating unforgettable characters in their songs, stories, and other works—to dramatize the satisfactions and problems of Catholic life in ways the clergy all too often fails to do. In this regard, they pose a special challenge to the Church, as democratically minded people so often do for non-democratic institutions. But they are also a potentially invaluable resource for strengthening spiritual bonds in a society often ambivalent about its secularity and hungry for models that are authoritative without being authoritarian.

If nothing else, I hope the book will provide a sliver of light in illuminating the vision of a wayward, but not disillusioned, American Catholic: that's how I see myself, and how I see a lot of my fellow Catholics. This search for light, and shared ground, is the essence of my own American Dream. I'm far from certain that it has any redeeming value. But then certainty has hardly been a prerequisite for any quest.

PART I

DEFINING THE DREAM

HEAVEN CAN WAIT

Scene from the triumphant ending of Italian Catholic director Frank
Capra's beloved 1946 film *It's a Wonderful Life*. Though not especially
popular at the time of its release (a matter to be discussed in chapter
six), the film has nevertheless long since become a Christmas favorite—
and a virtual compendium of American Dreams that include home
ownership, upward mobility, and a quest for "the good life." *(Photo
courtesy The Kobal Collection, New York)*

Chapter One

THE COMPLEXITIES OF THE AMERICAN DREAM

The American Dream is one of the most familiar—and powerful—phrases in our national lexicon. Jubilant athletes declaim it following championship games. Aspiring politicians invoke it as the basis of their candidacies. Otherwise sober businessmen cite achieving it as the goal of their enterprises. The term seems like both the most lofty as well as the most immediate component of an American identity, a birthright far more meaningful and compelling than terms like "democracy," "constitution," or even "United States."

And yet for all its seeming simplicity and appeal, the American Dream is also a very complicated concept. For one thing, the opportunities the phrase implies also impose costs all the more painful for rarely being recognized, much less discussed. The unfulfilled yearnings of Jimmy Stewart's character in *It's a Wonderful Life* are never quite erased by the movie's happy ending (a matter I'll return to later). The failure of countless social reforms in this country, which founder on the confidence of individual citizens that *they* will be the ones who overcome the odds and get rich, is one of the great themes of American politics. And we've all heard stories about celebrities who find themselves overwhelmed by the very success they so fiercely pursued—and attained.

But it's one thing to achieve your dream and find out it isn't quite what you expected. It's another to live with the uncertainty and frustration of striving without ever really knowing if you can actually get there. The American Dream would have no drama or mystique if it were a self-evident falsehood or a scientifically demonstrable fact. Ironically, ambiguity is the very source of its power. This is true even for those who fail outright, for it raises the question of *why* they fail: do they blame themselves, bad luck, or the unattainability of the objective?

One of the more surprising aspects of the American Dream is that the phrase is of modern origin. To be sure, some notion of the idea goes back a long way in American life; one clearly senses it, for example, in what Alexis de Tocqueville called "the charm of antici-pated success" in his classic two-volume study *Democracy in America*, published between 1835 and 1840. But the first clear reference to the American Dream as such comes from James Truslow Adams's 1931 book *The Epic of America*. In the epilogue of this one-volume narrative history, Adams describes it as "that dream of a land in which life should be better and richer and fuller for every man, with opportunity for each according to his ability or achievement." Adams considered the American Dream a national gift to world civilization, and wrote his book during the Great Depression to remind his fel-low Americans of the priceless value of their heritage. (It seems apropos to note here that the copy of the book I checked out of the Harvard College library was a 1941 wartime edition that belonged to an American officer participating in the Allied Expeditionary Force that landed at D-Day: the Dream functioned as an explanation for why we fought.) Ironically, Adams was denied his wish to use "The American Dream" as his title, because his publisher refused to let him: no one, he was told, would pay three dollars for a hardcover book about a dream.

Amazingly, no one has written a narrative history of the Ameri-can Dream. To be sure, there are plenty of books that are in some way about it; if you do a keyword search of the phrase in the catalog of Harvard library, you retrieve over 700 entries that use "American Dream" in the title. Most of these, however, focus on a specific topic (e.g., *Abraham Lincoln and the Economics of the American Dream; The American Dream and the Popular Novel; Race, Sports and the American Dream*). Moreover, these books typically invoke the term without any real attempt to define or use it with any precision.

Perhaps the very familiarity of the American Dream leads people to take it for granted: there's no need to define the meanings and uses of a term everyone presumably understands. But I think there's an additional explanation for this striking omission: there is, in fact, no one American Dream. Instead, there are many American Dreams. James Truslow Adams's invocation of "that dream of a land in which life should be better and richer and fuller for every man" may be fine as far as it goes, but the devil is in the details: just what does "better," "richer," and "fuller" *mean*?

The answers vary. Sometimes "better and richer and fuller" is defined in terms of money—one could almost believe this as the *only* definition—but there are others. Political power, educational opportunity, sexual expression: the list is endless. These answers have not only been available at any given time; they have also changed over time and competed at the same time for that highly variable, but seemingly timeless, concept we call "common sense."

Perhaps, then, it would be useful to enumerate some categories of the Dream more specifically:

The American Dream of Freedom: Freedom, of course, is a term that gets invoked even more frequently (and loosely) than American Dream. It also takes many forms—freedom *to* and freedom *from*; personal freedom and political freedom; public freedom and private freedom, and so on. Whatever the variety, though, freedom is an indispensable prerequisite for any American Dream: a dream can have vitality only if there is at least a theoretical sense of agency that allows one to pursue it, something that typically goes by the name of "opportunity."

That said, there is a general American Dream of Freedom that has been cited throughout U.S. history. As I'll be discussing in some detail in the next chapter, freedom in colonial America was fundamentally a religious idea, and the core of this very early American Dream involved the liberty to worship as one wished, a dream pursued by Puritans, Baptists, Quakers, and others amid resistance from the mother country.

Later, the Dream of Freedom took on a more political connotation in the struggles of the Founding Fathers to create the United States. The Declaration of Independence, with its clarion call for "life, liberty, and the pursuit of happiness," is the charter of the American Dream. Never before had the personal aspirations of individuals been named as a justification for a nation, and to this day it is precisely such aspirations that bring most people here.

The most powerful recent version of the Dream of Freedom—

one that, perhaps not surprisingly, fused both the religious and political components—was the Civil Rights Movement. Its greatest proponent was Martin Luther King, Jr., who specifically invoked the Dream throughout his career, most famously in his "I Have a Dream Speech" during the March on Washington in 1963. Ever since, King's name has been virtually synonymous with the American Dream of freedom.

Not all dreams of freedom have been as attractive, however. In many cases this is because, unlike King's, they separated freedom from equality. The Puritans, for example, were notorious for asserting their own religious freedom while denying it to anyone else. The Dred Scott Supreme Court decision of 1857 explicitly defined freedom as the right of white Americans to own black Americans, and the fear of losing this right led the South to fight for a dream of the Confederate States of America—one that lingers with striking vividness in examples that range from *Gone with the Wind* to the iconography of Dixie flags flying over state capitals.

Today, the Dream of Freedom is more commonly expressed as freedom *from*—from taxes, from government supervision, from responsibility for anyone other than oneself or one's kin. This is the dream of figures ranging from former Republican presidential candidate Steve Forbes to Oklahoma City bomber Timothy McVeigh. While the libertarian perspectives of such widely disparate figures lacks universal appeal—most of us define our social obligations more broadly than these otherwise very different people—one should not doubt the sincerity and intensity of those who view their brand of freedom as an unrealized, but realiz*able*, ideal.

Meanwhile, there remain alternatives that *do* define freedom in terms of equality. One senses this in a recent comment of my daycare provider, Padmini Amarasiri, a Sri Lankan immigrant who runs a center out of her home. "This was my dream," she said in accented English to my wife one recent weekday afternoon. Amarasiri referred not to starting a business or owning a home (both matters to be discussed shortly), but rather the right to participate in the public sphere—one conspicuously lacking for women in her native country—that made both possible. This Dream of Freedom, I suspect, has been both more and less than she expected, but there is little doubt of its ongoing centrality in her life. And in this, surely, she is not alone.

The American Dream of Upward Mobility: Like the Dream of Freedom, this one takes many forms. It finds expression in the familiar hope, typically associated with immigrants, that your children will enjoy a better standard of living than you. Here again, though, the issue is *which* standard. One of the most important is education, an institution Americans have embraced with unique energy. From the free public schools established in New York in the 1660s to land grant colleges chartered by Congress in the 1860s to the government loan and affirmation action programs of the 1960s, education has been widely viewed as the single most important vehicle for upward mobility in American life.

Few figures have expressed this faith in achieving the American Dream of upward mobility via education more vividly than the Russian Jewish immigrant Mary Antin. In her classic 1912 memoir *The Promised Land*, Antin movingly described how she was literally schooled in the Dream. "As I read how the patriots planned the Revolution, and the women gave their sons to die in battle, and the heroes led to victory, and the rejoicing people set up the Republic, it dawned on me gradually what was meant by *my country*," she wrote. "The people all desiring noble things, and striving for them together, defying their oppressors, giving their lives for each other—all this made it *my country*." Antin later went on to become a distinguished student, journalist, and activist who propounded education as the cornerstone of the American Dream.

But formal education has never been the sole means of upward mobility, even for those who acquired it. American history is rife with figures, from Benjamin Franklin (whose first published work satirized a Harvard he never attended) to Bill Gates (who dropped out of Harvard in his junior year) who were at best indifferent students but who nevertheless attained great stature and wealth in their lifetimes. The most common form of advancement was business, and much of the appeal of free enterprise has come from the belief that it too is an avenue—in some minds, *the* avenue—for achieving upward mobility.

This particular mythology was codified in the novels of Horatio Alger in the last third of the nineteenth century. In titles like *Strive and Succeed, Forging Ahead, Struggling Upward,* and others (they tend to run together after a while), Alger, a former Unitarian minister, depicted poor boys with few resources—other than common sense, a willingness to work, and a generous heart—who inevitably find their fortunes and win the hand of the boss's daughter. The formula has been reworked countless times since in works that range from *How to Succeed in Business Without Really Trying* and to the latest self–help exhortations from Anthony Robbins.

There is, however, a tension at the heart of the Dream of Upward Mobility. For all the tireless celebrations of hard work, it is almost never the only, or even primary, reason for success. When one looks carefully at the Alger novels, for example, pluck is trumped by luck. It's not the year-in, year-out drudgery that finally explains the young man's rise, but the instinct to rescue the girl who fell off the ferry (the one who turns out to be the boss's daughter), or the casual show of courtesy that impresses the rich man in search of a protégé. There have always been those who have argued that there is no contradiction here—to paraphrase Thomas Jefferson, the harder you work, the luckier you get—but chance is never allowed to overshadow effort in these versions of the American Dream. A focus on luck could cast real doubt on the efficiency and fairness of an ideal in which investments run very deep.

The American Dream of Home Ownership: In some sense, one could legitimately argue that home ownership is a variation on the Dream of Upward Mobility. Building or buying a house, after all, requires the kind of capital investment that is often the result of sustained labor, and Americans—who voluntarily relocate more than any non-nomadic people on earth—often replace modest homes for larger, more expensive ones. That said, upward mobility involves fundamentally different aspirations than home ownership: the former, by definition, involves movement and change; the latter involves a quest for stability, continuity, and permanence. Moreover, it's the *idea* of home ownership that matters more than any particular house a family may buy or sell. In this sense, home ownership is the flip side of upward mobility, a longing to settle that complements (or, as a heavily leveraged mortgage holder might observe here, *restrains*) an urge to escape. The tension between these two dreams is one of the great themes of American literature. Thomas Wolfe told us we can't go home again, and yet the traffic jams that surround our airports each Thanksgiving testifies to our refusal, in the face of much evidence to the contrary, to accept this assertion. The American Dream virtually *demands* a home, if only in a (sentimentalized) imagination.

A series of historical factors help explain the appeal of the American Dream of Home Ownership, which by the turn of the twenty-first century reached about two-thirds of American households—a record. The abundance of wood in North America compared with a long-deforested Europe made this critical raw material cheap and plentiful for the builders of log cabins. The development of balloon frame construction in Chicago in the 1830s—a technique that remains in use to this day— greatly accelerated home building and put it within reach of those without the time or talent to personally construct houses. Government policy was also important. The Homestead Act signed into law by President Lincoln in 1862 literally gave millions of Americans a stake in their country. The GI Bill subsidized the growth of the nation's suburbs after World War II by backing borrowers banks never would. And the right to deduct home-mortgage interest from taxable income—perhaps the single largest and most important government welfare program in contemporary American life—has in many cases literally made owning a home cheaper than renting one for those Americans capable of coming up with a down payment.

In our time, the most compelling figure in the Dream of Home Ownership is Abraham Levitt. Levitt and his sons William and Alfred had been relatively small-scale contractors before the Second World War, when they received a government contract to build over 2000 homes for war workers in Norfolk, Virginia. Returning to Long Island after the war, they acquired a 4000-acre tract of potato fields in the township of Hempstead. Their development, which was known at the time as Island Trees, was soon renamed Levittown.

The Levitts perfected a house-building formula inspired by assembly line practices. Trucks dropped off building materials at sixty-foot intervals. Freight cars delivered Levitt-owned timber to lumberyards, where one man could cut parts for ten houses in a day. Aided by new electrically powered tools, the houses were constructed in twenty-seven concrete steps by workers who specialized in particular jobs (right down to the color of the paint). Preassembled parts and appliances were provided by wholly owned subsidiaries, and the company used non-union labor, making up for rainy days on weekends. At the height of production, thirty houses went up a day. When complete, Levittown consisted of over 17,000 houses and 82,000 residents, making it the largest housing development ever built in the United States.

Here truly was an American Dream within reach of the masses. The Cape Cod-style homes, which were built in a few standard variations, typically offered about 750 square feet of space and were sold for as little as $6990 (including a washing machine). As little as ten percent was all that was necessary for a down payment, and because the mortgage, interest, principal and taxes were often less than rent, virtually all were owner-occupied—particularly since government aid in the form of Veterans Authority (VA) and Federal Housing Authority (FHA) guarantees allowed the Levitts both the capital to build the houses and freedom from risk in lending it. In the years that followed, they would build similar developments in Pennsylvania and New Jersey—and, more importantly, would be followed by a wave of similar development across the country. By the end of the twentieth century, suburbanites would outnumber both rural and city residents; no American Dream can compare to it in scope or in the number of people who have achieved it.

As always, there is a flip side to this dream—one present from the very beginning. Greed and deception denied minorities access to money, neighborhoods, and the legal recourse to do anything about it. Environmental recklessness leveled forests, polluted rivers, and destroyed species. The explicit FHA policy of redlining—i.e., declaring certain towns, cities, and neighborhoods with high minority populations too risky to insure—made them virtually worthless to banks and buyers. Levitt himself refused to sell to African Americans for fear that it would hurt his business. In this regard, of course, both he and the government simply reflected the attitudes of the voters and customers they served. "We can solve a housing problem, or we can try to solve a racial problem," Levitt explained in the isn't-it-obvious, commonsense logic of the early postwar years. "But we cannot combine the two." In 1960 not a single resident of Levittown was black. The tremendous achievements of the Dream of Home Ownership seem inextricable from its awful failures.

The American Dream of the Good Life: This is perhaps the most powerful of American dreams in contemporary national life—and the most insidious. All the other dreams described here are premised on the idea that their attainment is a matter of intense desire coupled with sustained exertion. Not so the Good Life. Draining its connotation of any moral dimension, "good" here simply means a sense of luxury, wealth, and fame, all of which are attained with seeming effortlessness. Talent may count, but that's not the focus: fun is. Imagine a glamorous actress laughingly describing her recent project on the living-room set of a television talk show, and you have some sense of what I mean by the dream of the Good Life. It's about succeeding in business without really even *having* to try. (This particular version of the Good Life, which I call the Dream of Celebrity, will be discussed further in chapter five, which looks at the role of Catholicism in Madonna's career.)

It is tempting to believe that the American Dream of the Good Life is of relatively recent vintage, or has become especially widespread at the end of the twentieth century. But this isn't really true. Decades before the Puritans came to New England in 1630, the Virginia Company landed in the South in search of profits from tobacco. Like all investors, these men—few of whom did the actual work of sailing, planting, or fighting—wanted to make money. But their mentality was more of gamblers than managers. Indeed, those who fret about government-sponsored gambling may be surprised to learn that lotteries were among the most important financial instruments in building colonial North America, not only in raising funds for initial settlement but also for homes, schools, and other community institutions. In fact, when the hoped-for profits did not materialize, King James I authorized the Virginia Company to use lotteries to help prop up its sagging investments overseas; those who bought tickets were known as "adventurers." In a larger sense, America itself was an enormous adventure for well over a century after the arrival of Captain John Smith; from the lowliest convict bound for Georgia to the richest merchant trading rum, molasses, and slaves in Newport, the colonies cultivated dreams of fast, easy prosperity.

This mentality remained an important facet of American life: for speculators (such as George Washington) who bought western land before it was entirely safe or legal to do so; for cardsharps on Mississippi riverboats looking for an easy mark on the way to New Orleans; for miners in the camps that sprang up in the wake of the California Gold Rush—all these were manifestations of the quest western writer Wallace Stegner once called "the big rock candy mountain" in the novel of the same name. The West in particular has been especially important in the elaboration of this particular American Dream, whose provincial capitals are Las Vegas and Hollywood. It is also alive and well in New York, where corporate executives orchestrate massive mergers, buyouts, and other multi-billion maneuvers that result in compensation—it's hard to even use the term with a straight face—that is literally beyond imagining.

The supreme figure in the Dream of the Good Life is Elvis Presley, a poor boy from rural Mississippi who literally became the voice of the American century as it approached its crest. Moving to the big city of Memphis as a child, he attracted the attention of a record producer for doing what he loved to do best: singing. From there, it was on to New York, Hollywood, and Vegas in an orgy of fame and wealth that brings pilgrims to the shrine of Graceland.

Although not known as an especially articulate man, Presley expressed his American Dream with notable clarity: "When I was a boy, I was the hero in comic books and movies. I grew up believing in a dream. Now I've lived it out. That's all a man can ask for." Ironically, as we know, it wasn't enough. For the world of comic books and movies is gossamer-thin, and Presley had trouble expressing, let alone finding, anything else to ask for. In a very real sense, his dream destroyed him.

But the insidiousness of this dream resides not only in its lack of substance, nor in the fact that its success stories are publicized out of all proportion to the number of people who actually live them. It is also that this particular dream has tended to corrupt others, either by casting doubts about their efficacy (like the pirate or gangster who regards the Dream of Freedom as irrelevant, if not stupid) or inculcating covetousness (a house is not really a home unless it has *x* number of bedrooms).

The truth is, though, that the line between this dream and the others can be slippery, even imperceptible. We tend to think positively of those who strike it rich by dint of hard work, but in what sense can one ever really *earn* one million dollars, never mind ten or one hundred million, a year? On the other hand, does anyone seriously question the legitimacy of considering the market value of a home—which can be used to finance an education or a retirement— as a major element of its appeal?

Whatever its particular contours, the American Dream has never been imagined as a zero-sum solution: the idea is to end up with more than you started. Or, to put it a little differently, the American Dream, whatever its specific form, rests on a belief that one—note the pronoun here, because individualism has typically been central— can achieve one's desires. Not *will* achieve, mind you, but *can* achieve: it's about a theoretical possibility that tantalizes, and actually happens just often enough to make it seem legitimate. Such fervent hopes are hardly a new phenomenon in human history. But no society has been collectively premised on them the way American society has.

Indeed, most societies have been based on very different premises. Sometimes such premises are secular, as in the glorification of a particular ruler, state, or empire. More often, though, such premises are religious—that is to say that they place at least some emphasis on an afterlife which, depending on one's behavior, holds the promise of a more rewarding existence in the next life (perhaps justifying martyrdom, or killing others in a holy war). And whether Hindu, Buddhist, Muslim, or any number of other faiths, most world religions specifically reject the core tenet of the American Dream: a belief that one can find true satisfaction in worldly pursuits. So do all varieties of Christianity.

How on earth, then, did the American Dream take root? Americans have never been an especially godless people. Actually, it's often said that they are the most religious people in the world (though I must say it's not clear what this means, other than perhaps the crude indicator of church attendance). Moreover, their piety has commonly been regarded as one with a long history; those of us who know next to nothing about the Pilgrims, for example, know that religion had a great deal to do with their coming to these shores. So how is it that such an insistently secular idea emerged from people who are regarded as having a strong sense of the sacred nature of human life?

The answer to this question begins with the Roman Catholic Church. Born at the height of the most successful earthly empire the world has ever known, and a persecuted cult in its formative stages, the Church began as a source of solace for disparaged outsiders, offering them the promise of a better world beyond the inevitable sorrows of this one. To be sure, the Church often exhibited an unseemly interest in, and desire for control over, earthly affairs, particularly in the first half of the last millennium, when its political power was at its height. But there has never been any question of its role as a haven in a heartless world that will always frustrate even the best-intentioned mortal designs.

Beginning in about 1500, the Catholic Church faced a powerful challenge in the form of the Protestant Reformation. While one should be careful in making broad remarks about Protestantism in general and the Reformation in particular (any label that describes both an Assembly of God evangelical and a Unitarian agnostic, for example, obscures more than it reveals), it does seem useful to note the very etymological basis of the word "Reformation": reform. For all their variety, Protestants have historically shared a belief that the Catholic Church, like all mortal institutions, was seriously flawed. But they went one step further to believe they could nevertheless do better. *How* they could do better, and how *much* better has been open to much debate—thus the seemingly endless fragmentation *within* Protestantism. But a sense of confidence that this world could be improved, and that its improvement might have a real relationship with salvation in the next one, has been a central feature of the Protestant experience. In the immediate aftermath of the Reformation, some elements in the Catholic Church—one thinks here of the

Jesuits—jumped on the reform bandwagon. Still, the reformist impulse remains an important and defining feature in the sprawling world of Protestantism even today.

Of course, reform was only one factor impelling the Reformation. To cite one ultimately significant example: King Henry VIII of England—a man dubbed "Defender of the Faith" by Pope Leo X— was initially appalled by the uproar caused when Martin Luther nailed his Ninety-five Theses on a church door in Wittenburg in 1517. But the breach proved convenient for him seventeen years later when he couldn't get the divorce he wanted, and his creation of the Church of England (or Anglican Church) proved to be both politically popular and financially rewarding for him and his heirs.

Amid the religious conflicts that would dominate England for the next century and a half, there was a small minority of Anglican subjects—a splinter of a splinter, in effect—which grew increasingly disenchanted by the lack of rigor and commitment in the Church of England. Skeptical they could reform it from within, and subject to increasing persecution, they began to dream of leaving England altogether and beginning all over again in a new world they would remake in their own image. Freed from the corruption of European power politics, they would make a City of God, coming as close as any human beings ever have to creating a heaven on earth. They began climbing on boats in 1620.

What happened to their dream when they got off those boats— and what happened to the dreams of those who got off those boats after them—is the subject of the next chapter. Before concluding this one, though, two major points need to be addressed. First, while we today typically think of the American Dream as a secular idea (something I have devoted some space here to describing), its origins are fundamentally religious: once the "good" life really did mean *good* in the truest sense of that term. Second, the American Dream was not really a Catholic idea. In fact, it was something of an *anti*-Catholic idea, a reality that would have tremendous consequences for Catholic and non-Catholic alike for the next 300 years. I plan to explore this concept more fully in the next chapter.

IN HONOR OF THE BIRTHDAY OF GOVERNOR JOHN WINTHROP, BORN JUNE 12, 1587.

PURELY ANTI-CATHOLIC

An 1854 illustration honoring John Winthrop, govenor of Massachusetts twelve times between 1630 and 1649. Symbolically situated between a Puritan and an Indian, and presiding over a settlement he once famously described as a "city on a hill," Winthrop helped establish a colony in the New World specifically predicated on offering an alternative to "papal" influences in England as well as rival Catholic powers France and Spain. *(Photo from the Collections of the Library of Congress)*

Chapter Two

THE ANTI-CATHOLIC ORIGINS
OF THE AMERICAN DREAM

. . . This Afternoons Entertainment was to me most awfull and affecting. The poor Wretches fingering their Beads, chanting Latin, not a Word of which they understood; their Pater Nosters and Ave Marias. Their holy Water—their Crossing themselves perpetually—their Bowing to the Name of Jesus, whenever they hear it—their Bowings, Kneelings, and genuflections before the Altar. The Dress of the Priest was rich with Lace—his pulpit was Velvet and Gold. The Altar Piece was very rich—little Images and Crucifixes about—Wax Candles lighted up. But how shall I describe the Picture of our Saviour in a Frame of Marble over the Altar, at full Length, upon the Cross in the Agonies, and the Blood dropping and streaming from his Wounds!

The Musick, consisting of an Organ and a Choir of singers, went all the Afternoon excepting sermon Time, and the Assembly chanted—most sweetly and exquisitely.

Here is everything which can charm and bewitch the simple and the ignorant. I wonder how Luther ever broke the spell.

—John Adams on a Catholic service he attended
with George Washington during the First Continental
Congress in Philadelphia, October 1774

In the beginning, America was a Catholic domain. Perhaps you remember the standard history as you learned it in school: Genoan sailor Christopher Columbus made his first journey across the Atlantic Ocean in 1492, and bumped into the so-called New World—which, we've frequently since been reminded, was neither new nor a world—

while seeking a maritime passage to China. He claimed his discoveries for the fledgling Spanish empire of King Ferdinand and Queen Isabella, who financed his expedition. In 1493 Pope Alexander VI arbitrated a dispute between Spain and her main imperial rival, Portugal, by dividing the Atlantic world between them. This so-called Line of Demarcation allocated virtually all the land in the contested zone to Spain, though Portuguese dissatisfaction with the arrangement led in 1494 to the Treaty of Tordesillas, which gave Portugal the territory that later became Brazil. Other European powers were not happy to be excluded from negotiations over the future of the New World, but at this point there was little they could do about it.

The name "America" was coined in 1507 by German cartographer Martin Waldseemüller, who derived it from Americus, a Latinized version of the name of Italian navigator Amerigo Vespucci. Originally, "America" referred specifically to islands of the Caribbean Sea and the northeastern coast of what we now call South America. The term was first used to denote the entire western hemisphere in 1538 on a map published by Flemish geographer Geradus Mercator. Spain and Portugal dominated the hemisphere for a century after Columbus's arrival; in 1608, Samuel de Champlain arrived in modern-day New Brunswick, Canada, and claimed it for France, marking the beginning of a new phase of colonial struggle.

Again: all of these colonizers were Catholic powers. (France, which had been rent by religious strife for much of the early Reformation, emerged from the sixteenth century with Catholics in charge and Protestants scattered to the winds.) For all their differences, and for all their secular striving, each assigned themselves evangelical responsibilities for propagating the faith. Hernan Cortés, conqueror of the Aztecs, always carried an icon of the Virgin Mary; he prayed and heard mass daily, and the standard his troops carried bore the words "Comrades, with true faith we follow the sign of the Holy Cross and through it we shall conquer."

The legendary brutality of Cortés, which typified European colonial policy in America, makes it difficult to view European evangelical efforts among natives with much enthusiasm. And the resilience of Native American folkways and religions—the highly adaptable tenor of Pueblo life, for example, or the tendency for French fur traders to adopt Huron religions—make clear that theological communication with the inaccurately labeled "Indians" was not a one-way street. Still, it was evident by 1600 that while the Vatican did not have complete supremacy over the entire New World, its grip extended far and wide. And while its hold on North America, a desolate frontier considered less valuable than the golden riches of the Caribbean islands or Mexico, was tenuous, it had nevertheless established a presence in a vast arc that encompassed Quebec, Florida, and (just barely) California.

It would be hard to overestimate the importance of these realities as a prelude to discussing my main focus here, namely British North America and what became the United States of America. In 1600 England was still a minor, if rising, power in the Atlantic world, a wily opportunist loosely allied with other Protestant nations that spent much of the era on the military, if not religious, defensive. English involvement in America was focused on preying on Spanish shipping in the Caribbean, hoping to shake loose some of the gold that traveled between Spain's colonies and the mother country.

Yet even the most naked greed was not without religious implications. Take, for example, the case of the Cimarrons, a group of about 3000 escaped slaves who raided Spanish settlements from their base in present–day Panama. In 1572 Sir Francis Drake, the notorious pirate, slave trader, and favorite of Queen Elizabeth I of England, landed on the coast to capture a Spanish mule train of loot making its way across the isthmus from the Pacific to the Caribbean side. Having arrived too early to intercept the treasure, Drake made an alliance with the Cimarrons and eventually succeeded in jointly capturing a fortune in gold and silver. A few years later, Drake's lieutenant, John Oxenham, was back on the isthmus with fifty men. By early 1577 Cimarron-English guerrillas were raiding Spanish shipping from Peru—and, while they were at it, made a point of desecrating Catholic churches by smashing images, altars, and crucifixes. Spanish authorities reported that the Cimarrons had become enthusiastic "Lutherans" (the Spanish umbrella term for all Protestants), to the point of crying "I English; pure Lutheran" during their raids. They even exhorted their victims not to believe in the Holy Trinity or in the divinity of Mary.

This particular military/racial/religious alliance collapsed when Oxenham was captured and hanged. Drake himself, who wandered as far as the coast of northern California, was typically more interested in buying and selling African slaves than in forging economic and cultural exchanges with them. But the Cimarron episode and others like it were regarded as promising evidence that England could establish permanent bases in the New World, and in so doing establish viable alternatives to Spanish government as well as religion in the process.

The first such enterprise was the so-called lost colony of Roanoke, explored in 1584 by men with another Elizabethan pirate, Sir Walter Raleigh. The emphasis here is on the word *enterprise:* from the very beginning, Roanoke (which English travelers found abandoned upon their return about five years later) and the subsequent settlement of the Virginia Company in Jamestown in 1607 were undertakings heavily motivated by economic considerations.

Yet, as in other cases, sectarian factors were deeply entwined with secular undertakings. The official religion of Virginia, named for its virgin queen, was the Church of England, or Anglican Church. Primitive frontier conditions—among them social isolation, high death rates, and a shortage of clergy—made it difficult to think of religion as much more than a formality. Still, the mere fact that Virginia was created as an English charter company had important sectarian implications: because of the decisions made by Henry VIII about seventy-five years earlier, *English* meant *Protestant.* This did not mean, though, that everyone quietly accepted (or quietly ignored) official religious authorities; England, like all major European powers, also had to deal with vocal minorities at home and abroad. Nor did it mean that the government itself was conscientious about upholding religious orthodoxy. Throughout the Western world, Christian political leaders shared interests that were not necessarily identical to those of their church leaders. Nevertheless, if religion was no longer the decisive force it had once been in European affairs, it was nevertheless a factor that could have unpredictable—and powerful—consequences.

There is no better example of this unpredictable power than the attitudes and actions of a relatively small group of Anglican dissidents who emerged in the late sixteenth century. Although not always united in their geographic or theological outlook, they were nevertheless notable for their spiritual rigor and ambition, which to outsiders seemed excessively grim and moralistic. The word associated with these people—a word that was both loosely applied and meant to be unflattering—was "Puritan." "We call you Puritans, not because you are purer than other men . . . but because you think yourselves to be purer," an English clergyman wrote in the early seventeenth century.

The name, and the image, stuck. Even now, those of us who know virtually nothing about American history have a fairly clear, even vivid, picture of seventeenth-century Puritans as joyless martinets who were even more prudish about sex than twentieth-century Irish Catholics. Writers from Nathaniel Hawthorne to H. L. Mencken have viewed the Puritans as the source of all the defects in American society; in Mencken's famous formulation, Puritanism is "the haunting fear that someone, somewhere, may be happy." The poor image of the Puritans got a new lease on life in the postwar era with the premiere of Arthur Miller's 1953 play *The Crucible*, which rounded out this portrait by emphasizing the mindless conformity and hypocrisy of Puritan life. Even now, observers both here and abroad who scratched their heads over the brouhaha surrounding the Clinton-Lewinsky scandal of the 1990s often attribute what they consider an otherwise inexplicable obsession with sex to the nation's Puritan heritage.

The historical perception of the Puritans has long been hardened into stereotype. Like all people lumped into groups, the Puritans were in fact complicated human beings whose thought and behavior was laced with countercurrents and irrational practices that were both historically specific and timeless. To be sure, they had plenty to answer for. But for the purposes of this discussion, a focus on their defects is less important than noting this: They had a dream.

Of course, lots of people in world history have had dreams; it's one of the things that makes human beings human. Certainly the Spanish, French, Portuguese, and other adventurers in America had aspirations of their own, which typically involved extracting riches from the edge of the world. Catholic missionaries from all these nations had dreams of converting Indians. And the Indians had dreams of their own; wishing these foreigners would go away was surely prominent among them.

What the Puritans wanted, however, was a little unusual: to start over. They sought to do this not simply on an individual basis, or as a matter of organizing heathens on a civilized model, but in actually building a city of God in the wilderness for themselves. This project might involve making money (something we know the Puritans proved to be very good at), and it might involve converting Indians (something the Puritans were notably less successful at than Spanish or even French missionaries). But neither was finally as important to them as remaking *their* world on a more spiritually satisfying basis in a place they could call truly their own.

This ambition did not take form all at once. By the end of the sixteenth century, some Anglican dissidents, subject to persecution and appalled by the spiritual slackness around them, gave up hope that they could ever be at home in England, and formally left the Church of England—hence their designation as Separatists. Some went to Holland, where a successful struggle to achieve independence from Spanish Catholic rule inspired the belief that they might find a true holy land. Yet here too they were disappointed. The most far-sighted of these Separatists "began both deeply to apprehend their present dangers [of moral corruption] and wisely to foresee the future and think of a timely remedy," wrote William Bradford in his classic history *Of Plymouth Plantation*. "In the agitation of their thoughts, and much discourse of things hereabout, they began to incline to this conclusion: of removal to some other place."

That place, of course was, America. Financed by a group of London investors, the Pilgrims boarded the *Mayflower*, intending to settle in Virginia. Like many Atlantic travelers, they went astray, and instead landed on a piece of North Atlantic coastline that had never been regarded as especially attractive by any European explorers. It was there, a place they named Plymouth in honor of a city in their homeland, that they took their stand, and elected Bradford their leader.

Most of those who made the journey were Separatists—or, as they came to be known, Pilgrims. However, some were not, and these people sought to separate from the Separatists. To prevent this, Pilgrim leaders wrote the so-called Mayflower Compact, a civil document modeled after the covenant that had established their religious faith. Each male adult signed the document, agreeing to follow all "just and equal" laws that the settlers enacted, and to be ruled by the will of the majority. Thus was laid one of the first foundations of American democracy.

Meanwhile, another group of dissidents—these were *non*-Separating Anglicans who hoped to reform the church from *within*—were making their own plans. Relatively affluent and sophisticated, they requested a charter for a corporation, the Massachusetts Bay Company, which would provide the financial incentive for investors to support still another English colony. In granting their request, the government took it for granted that the meetings of the corporation would take place in a major English city, such as London, and thus remain under close supervision of the Crown. But the charter for the Massachusetts Bay Company stipulated no such meeting place, a seeming oversight that was very much by design. For the company planned to hold its meetings in America, beyond the reach of royal authority. When, as hoped, the government approved the charter without noticing this omission, Massachusetts in effect became a society in its own right from the moment its members landed on the rocky New England coast in 1630. It quickly overshadowed Plymouth in size and influence, and eventually absorbed it (in 1691).

The goals of these ambitious spiritual pilgrimages were described most vividly by John Winthrop in his famous lay sermon "A Model of Christian Charity." Winthrop, one of the organizers of the Massachusetts Bay Company, was chosen by its colonists to govern them, a post he was subsequently elected to twelve times. Winthrop delivered his sermon on board the *Arbella*, one of four ships that carried about seven hundred immigrants across the Atlantic Ocean. Though its precise content is not certain (it was not published in his lifetime), it captures both the world the Puritans longed for and the world they inhabited.

In some ways, "A Model of Christian Charity" is a document of hardheaded realism. "God Almighty in his holy and wise providence hath so disposed the condition of mankind, as in all times some must be rich, some poor, some high and eminent and power and duty, others mean and in subjection," Winthrop began. God, he explained, ordered these differences "for the preservation and good of the whole," and exhorted the Puritans to maintain that order. Winthrop, like most Puritan leaders, affirmed sacred and secular hierarchy in government.

And yet the heart of the sermon was a call for interdependence, even equality, for all Puritans in the eyes of God. "No man is made more honorable than another or more wealthy, etc., out of any particular and singular respect to himself, but for the glory of his creator and the common good of the creature, man," he asserted. Like the different components of an organism that work in complementary effort to sustain it, Winthrop invoked a communitarian vision of American life: "We must delight in each other, make others' condition our own, rejoice together, mourn together, labor and suffer together, always having before our eyes our commission and community in the work, our community as members of the same body."

Such soaring hopes co-existed with mundane, even gnawing realities. At first glance, one of the more surprising things about "A Model of Christian Charity" is the amount of space it devotes to financial matters. In the highly structured interrogative style typical of Puritan sermons, Winthrop poses a series of questions—How should one determine how much money one gives to charity? What rules should govern lending?—that he answers in some detail. (In the case of the latter, for example, one should assess the odds of repayment, and if likely, lend what is asked, and if not, give only what is essential.) Of course, ever since Max Weber's classic study *The Protestant Ethic and the Spirit of Capitalism* in 1918, associations between Puritans and their money have been common, and rightly so. But what is sometimes overlooked is the intense ambivalence, even hostility, toward a market economy the Puritans felt even as they plunged into it. Winthrop was only one of many landholders in the late sixteenth and early seventeenth centuries to be impaled on the horns of a painful dilemma: inflationary pressures for rising rents conflicted with feudal injunctions for landlords to deal paternalistically with tenants. Some made the transition to the new economy; others lost their fortunes to their overseers. Winthrop was one of a few who dealt with the problem by emigrating to America. In this context, a call for communitarian cooperation was less cheap sentiment than a utopian wish forged on an anvil of pressing economic conditions.

Moreover, the threat of failure looms large over "A Model of Christian Charity." Winthrop's closing call has often been cited as a source of inspiration, most recently by President Ronald Reagan: "For we must consider that we shall be as a city upon a hill." Yet in the context of his sermon, the city on the hill was less a metaphor for a shining example for others to follow than a potential object of ridicule. "The eyes of all people are upon us, so that if we shall deal falsely with our God in this work we have undertaken, and so cause him to withdraw his present help from us, we shall be made a story and a byword through the world," Winthrop wrote. "We shall open the mouths of enemies to speak evil of the ways of God, and all professors for God's sake. We shall shame the faces of many of God's worthy servants, and cause their prayers to be turned into curses upon us till we be consumed out of the good land whither we are agoing."

Still, is there really anything all that remarkable about what Winthrop says in "A Model of Christian Charity?" In one sense, no. Most of the sentiments in the sermon would have been unexceptional had they been uttered by an archbishop in a Roman cathedral. Actually, the emphasis on hierarchical social organization, communal values, and the responsibilities of the privileged to the underprivileged could have come from any parish priest. What is significant here is not much content as *context*: these words were *not* uttered by a clergyman in the church; they came from a layman on a ship full of people trying to put as much distance—literally as well as figuratively—as possible from a Catholic clergyman *and* a church. The Puritans may have regarded their "errand into the wilderness" as a principled act of conscience, but an archbishop would no doubt have viewed it as a monstrous demonstration of arrogance.

And make no mistake: for Winthrop and the rest of the Puritans, "the mouths of enemies" included those of reactionary papists. Actually, it would not be too much to suggest that for many Protestants in the sixteenth and seventeenth centuries, the pope served a

function similar to that of Adolf Hitler for Americans in the twentieth: a yardstick by which to measure evil. (The famed Protestant
theologian John Calvin referred to the pope as the anti-Christ in his
writings.) Despite the fact that Catholic communities of any consequence were hundreds, if not thousands, of miles away from
Massachusetts, denunciations of the Church came instinctively to
New England. Anne Bradstreet, the prodigiously talented Puritan
poet, remains well known for her marvelous meditations on faith,
marriage, and children. Less well known is her 1642 book *The Tenth
Muse*, in which she lashes out at Rome in fairly standard anti-Catholic
imagery:

> These are the days the Church [of England]'s foes to crush,
> To root out Popelings head, tail, branch and rush;
> Let's bring Baal's vestments forth to make a fire,
> Their miters, surplices, and all their tire,
> Copes, rochets, crosiers, and such empty trash,
> And let their names consume, but let the flash
> Light Christendom, and all the world to see
> We hate Rome's whore, with all her trumpery.

Bradstreet's emphasis on the visual extravagance of the Catholic ritual typified much of the Puritan (and more generally Protestant)
hostility toward it. And the political context of her poem—which
was published as the English Civil War, very much a war of religion,
was getting underway—reflects the embattled posture of the Puritans, who were fighting a papal-leaning Stuart monarchy in their
homeland and suppressing the heresies of other Protestant sects
(among them Anabaptists and Quakers who had left Europe for the
same reasons the Puritans did) in New England.

Amid all the politics and petty venality that characterized so
much of the civil strife in the Atlantic world of the time, you might
well wonder how much of a real theological difference there was
between Puritans and Catholics. The answer is: enough to be significant. Although it is sometimes difficult to understand some of the
distinctions that separated the two sects, the doctrinal premises of
Puritanism were not only distinctive, but of major consequence for

the direction of future American culture, and the dreams that continue to animate it. That is why it would make some sense to explore them here.

Perhaps the first thing that needs to be said is that Puritanism belonged to the Calvinist branch of Protestantism. Calvinists, who were followers of the French-born Swiss theologian John Calvin (1509–1564) believed individuals' fates were sealed from the moment they were born, and there was absolutely nothing they could do to affect their ultimate salvation or damnation. But they could not know for sure where they were actually headed, and so had to live their lives hoping for signs that things would turn out for the best. To at least some extent, Calvinists were reacting to one of the most important reasons for the Protestant Reformation in the first place: the Roman Catholic practice of selling indulgences whereby the rich could buy forgiveness of their sins. What made indulgences so repellent was not so much what might bother someone today—a kind of class inequality evident that suggested salvation went to the highest bidder—but rather the implication that any human being could exercise prerogatives that belonged to God alone. For a committed Puritan, it was offensive to believe that an ordinary sinner could somehow move the levers of destiny.

Of course, living without any sense of, or control over, one's destiny was extremely difficult, even for someone who was not inclined to undertake gigantic tasks (like transatlantic migration) that might—or might not—result in religious salvation. And so the Puritans did something that many people do when trying to come to terms with challenging, even contradictory, ideas: they sought a middle ground. For them, this middle ground was known as the doctrine of *preparationism*. It was out of the question that one could directly affect one's fate through specific actions such as prayer or penance, since it smacked of a "doctrine of works" that already had corrupted Catholicism. But the doctrine of works was not only Catholic; it was also espoused by the Dutch theologian Jacobus Arminius and the much hated William Laud, the Bishop of London who persecuted Puritans in the name of the Church of England. On the other hand, to live a life whereby what one *felt* mattered far more than what one *did*, and which insisted on the impossibility of ever predicting who would be saved—a doctrine known as the "covenant of grace"—was for many Puritans too much to bear, for it meant that anyone, even an old drunkard, could stumble into heaven while even the most devout minister could be headed down a road to hell paved with good intentions. Preparationism, by contrast, softened the covenant of grace by suggesting that there were steps one could take to get in a proper frame of mind so that one could be fully receptive to sanctification should it be forthcoming.

If the message you're getting here comes across a little fuzzy, it's not you: it's Puritanism sending mixed signals. Despite a highly elaborate and formal pattern Puritan ministers used to instruct their congregations (who themselves must have been confused at least some of the time), the line between preparationism and the doctrine of works it sought to avoid seems gossamer–thin. Eventually, the Puritan emphasis on grace gradually wore down, and by the nineteenth century most American Protestants were frankly proclaiming a belief that individuals did, in fact, have a role to play in their salvation, a prominent feature of contemporary evangelical Protestantism in the United States. But this is getting a bit ahead of the story, and perhaps makes the Puritans seem stranger than they actually were in the context of their times.

Indeed, despite the widespread and generally accurate perception that the Puritans were radicals in the world of early modern Protestantism, the doctrine of preparationism is an important indication of their instinctive moderation. One sees this in the devious way the Massachusetts Bay Company went about securing its charter, which amounted to a bid for independence without an explicit declaration. One sees it, too, in the way Massachusetts Bay never formally reneged its ties to the Church of England until almost twenty years after the colony was chartered, when they joined with the Separatists of Plymouth and codified what came to be known as the Congregational Church.[1] And one sees it again in their less-than-intimate relationship between Plymouth and Massachusetts with the mother country in the English Civil War of the 1640s, a war that threatened to make the colonial errand into the wilderness irrelevant because a *reformed* England would make a *New* England unnecessary. That such pragmatism—some might say cynicism—could co-exist with their rigorous ideology suggests that these were flesh-and-blood people who lived lives that were very different than, and yet comparable to, our own. They made compromises in pursuit of what they wanted, and what they wanted often caused them a good deal of grief (as one Puritan scholar has pointed out, preparationism may well have increased rather than allayed anxiety, because it effectively ratcheted up expectations that Puritans *would* prepare rather than simply wait to see what happened).

By this point, you may be asking yourself: Why devote so much attention to an obscure religious doctrine that's now of little interest to anyone other than religious historians? The answer is that preparationism is indicative of a tendency important to the shaping of American national character: a desire for self-improvement most obvious in an American embrace of education (especially self-help). Paradoxically, the Calvinist assertion that one's salvation was solely in God's hands led to a notable commitment on the part of Puritans and their heirs to do all they could to maximize their chances. Thus it was that Harvard College was founded in a virtual wilderness in 1636, a mere six years after the Puritans arrived. Despite its place as a remote outpost of civilization, colonial New England had one of the highest literacy rates in the world (and its above–average education levels are routinely cited as the region's most important economic and social asset to this day).

American Catholics weren't as likely to link their earthly and heavenly fates in quite this way. This may be one reason, for example, why nineteenth- and early twentieth-century Irish and Italian Catholics were more likely to pin their hopes for upward mobility on owning land than sending their children to school the way Protestants and Jews—whose experience with centuries of discrimination had engendered a well–founded skepticism about the safety of assets they did not carry around in their heads—often did. These are, of course, loose generalizations; over time many Catholics did make often heroic efforts to educate their children, and religion was not the only—or, over time, the primary—reason Protestants and Jews pursued an education. Still, the Puritan desire for an *instructed* conscience proved to be an important factor in the evolution of American culture for the next three centuries.

This belief in the efficacy of education was part and parcel of another important personality trait: individualism. Here again was a force that had liturgical implications as well as important consequences for life beyond church walls, and long after church walls came down. As the Anne Bradstreet poem quoted earlier suggests, Protestants were disdainful toward elaborate ritual and the ornamentation that accompanied Catholic worship. Instead, they placed a special emphasis on the Bible as the word of God, as well as a special emphasis on each person having access to the word, not only in terms of literacy, but also in ensuring widespread distribution of the gospel. For no one was this more true than the Puritans (the first American printing press was established at Harvard in 1638). Without actually saying that the two were mutually exclusive, one might say the characteristic act of piety for a Catholic was participation in a communal Mass, while that of a Protestant was solitary reflection on Scripture. While a Catholic parish church was conceptualized as a vertically organized body that was part of a hierarchical worldwide organization, a Puritan congregation was a horizontally organized unit that chose and paid its own clergy and exercised complete autonomy over its management. When there were disagreements, factions would often split off and form their own churches—which is how, for example, the future state of Connecticut was founded by Puritan offshoots a mere five years after the landing at Massachusetts Bay. Thus, the Congregational Church was more loosely affiliated than other Protestant sects, such as the Presbyterian Church (organized by the clergy of a particular district) or the Anglican Church (organized by a regional grouping, or episcopacy, of bishops, hence the the Church of England in America became known as the Episcopalian Church).

The intensely local character of Congregational churches was reflected in the civic dimension of Puritan life. Though they were hardly paragons in separating church and state as we would understand the concept, the Puritans tended to stress the primacy of the individual conscience in everyday life. I've already mentioned the Mayflower Compact as a forerunner of democracy for the Pilgrims of Plymouth. The key contribution of Massachusetts Bay was the town meeting, in which members of a community could vote on matters of concern to them, and elect representatives to voice their concerns to the colony as a whole. As a practical matter, the king and parliament were too far away to make a practical difference in day-to-day life. To an unprecedented degree, then, this part of the world was virtually self-governing. And if you didn't like it, you could always leave—go west, for example. In this regard, you might say, the American Revolution began in the 1620s, not the 1770s, a time when some colonists were motivated more by freedoms they feared *losing* than gaining.

The Puritans tried to make the most of their unprecedented opportunities to make a city on a hill. In effect, this could mean the opposite of democracy as we've come to know it: New England was to be a place by, for, and of the Puritans, who, like others before and since, also proved to be world-class persecutors of people like the Quakers. That's not to say they were altogether intolerant of outsiders; the best shipwrights, for example, were not necessarily true believers, and there was always the possibility of Indians to convert, visitors to entertain, or even colonial officials to appease. But the clerical and civil leaders of both Plymouth and Massachusetts Bay planned to be in charge in both sacred and secular realms, which, while separate, were nevertheless intertwined. No one could join their churches without giving convincing public testimony of their "conversion" to Christ (admitting children solely on the basis of infant baptisms was viewed as typical Catholic laxity).[2] And only those who belonged to a congregation could vote in secular matters. Religious toleration of other sects was out of the question: these people had not come all that distance to accept the sloth, conflict, or obvious evil that had marred the corrupt old world they had left. From now on, they would cut through all the clutter and cacophony: no more ornate iconography in churches; no more decadent amusements like plays and gambling; even holidays like Christmas were unnecessary, idolatrous distractions. Long-standing attitudes could finally become official policy. A cherished dream was palpably within reach.

But from the start, things began to go astray. More accurately, people began to go astray, not so much in a spiritual sense (though some surely said and felt so) than in a literal one: the Puritans diffused over a much wider area than a compact city, and ended up in plains and valleys as well as upon hills. The Pilgrims first anchored at the tip of Cape Cod, and eventually settled further west in Plymouth, spreading out from there. The settlers of Massachusetts were even more itinerant. Their first encampment was at the present-day town of Salem, then at Charlestown, then a scattering across Watertown, Roxbury, Dorchester, Medford, and Saugus before concentrating in the peninsula known as Shawmut, which was ultimately named Boston for the East Anglian port city in England. By 1634 settlers were leaving Massachusetts Bay altogether and moving into New Haven and Hartford, laying the foundations for what would ultimately become Connecticut. Puritans also infiltrated New Hampshire, overwhelming the Anglican population there. The lust for land, the fear of contagious disease, and, one surmises, a desire for freedom from the burden of community, impelled this dispersal, which leaders like Winthrop regularly lamented. But expressions of regret, however sincere, did little to concentrate the spread of people who would go on to exhibit a seemingly inexhaustible appetite for frontiers.

Much of the social conflict in early New England centered on just how far to take the philosophical tenets of Puritanism, particularly in Massachusetts. The inhabitants' initial unwillingness to break publicly with the Anglican Church necessitated compromises that the Separatists of Plymouth, for example, did not feel compelled to make. Some Puritans considered such compromises as unacceptable forms of hypocrisy.

The most famous of these malcontents was Roger Williams. Williams came to Massachusetts in 1631, a generally well-liked figure with strong ministerial credentials. But his refusal to serve as pastor for a Boston congregation because it had not severed its ties with the Church of England was only the first of a series of declarations—among them assertions that the Puritans had acted illegally in acquiring land from the Indians—that at first worried, and finally infuriated, colonial officials so much so that they banished him from the colony altogether in 1636. Williams fled to what became known as Rhode Island, for which he received a royal charter, over Massachusetts' objections, in 1644. Rhode Island has been long known and remembered as a haven of toleration and relatively good Indian-settler relations, developments for which Williams deservedly gets credit. It's worth noting, however, that the impetus for Williams's ministry career was less an embrace of pluralism for its own sake than a refusal to allow what he regarded as the pollution of his religious practice—temperamentally he belonged, in effect, to a congregation of one.

One of the most serious challenges to the Puritan project was the so-called Antinomian crisis of the mid-1630s, the episode that more than any other suggested the practical limits of Puritan theory. Antinomians insisted that since no one knew who was saved, no one—not even ministers—could possess the religious authority to tell someone else what to think or do. At the heart of the Antinomian movement was a disgust with formulaic Puritan religious practices such as preparationism, which critics charged led people to lapse into empty rituals and cheap rationalizations that veered dangerously close to the Catholicism they rebelled against. Instead, they called for a rigorous, but deeply personal, approach to piety.

Taken to its logical conclusions, however, Antinomianism had deeply subversive implications. After all, the line between principled individualism and anarchic hedonism can be very thin: if every decision is personal, then who's to tell anyone else what's right or wrong? Moreover, even if one assumes that people would not turn into amoral animals if left to their own devices, it was only a matter of time before an individual's beliefs would lead to the rejection of civic as well as clerical authority, since most secular laws can be described as immoral for one reason or another. In maintaining that faith was *all* that mattered, Antinomianism went *beyond* Puritanism, falling into the fiercely egalitarian theology of the Quakers, for example, who had no ministers and relied on a silent dialogue between man and God. And the Quakers, as any devout Puritan would tell you, were thoroughly beyond the pale.

The most vocal proponent of Antinomianism was Anne Hutchinson. Hutchinson was an exceptionally charismatic and socially well-connected figure in early Massachusetts Bay. But suspicions about her activities and ties to the more radical wing of the congregation ultimately led to her being put on trial for "traducing the ministers and their ministry." The sole surviving transcript shows her to be an agile defendant, able to invoke Scripture with the best of her male adversaries. But when she claimed that she knew Scripture was correct because God had spoken to her directly about its veracity, she handed her opponents the means to brand her a heretic and banish her from the colony. She and her followers fled to Rhode Island and ultimately to New York, where she was killed by Indians near the river (and later highway) that today bears her name. From that point on, Puritanism retreated from the more controversial implications of its doctrines.

Ironically, even apparent *agreement* could create problems for the Puritans. New England prospered throughout the 1630s, as a steady arrival of disaffected Englishmen and Englishwomen found refuge and developed the local and even international economy of the region. But the onset of the English Civil War, a war waged and won by Oliver Cromwell's Puritans, created multiple problems for New England in the following decade. Wartime disruptions precipitated an economic recession, as the stream of new arrivals and the flow of goods slowed to a trickle. This ebbing also engendered what might be termed a psychological trauma: once an alternative beacon for discouraged English Puritans, New England now seemed irrelevant at best—and a self–indulgent sideline at worst—to some on *both* sides of the Atlantic. Puritans rejoiced at the execution of the much–hated Bishop Laud, but in some ways it was easier maintaining independence with an avowedly hostile British crown than a Puritan dictatorship seeking to centralize its administration and wary of New England's independence. Perhaps fortuitously, Cromwell's death in 1658 was followed by the restoration of the Stuart monarchy in 1660, and the New England Puritans returned to a situation where they were ruled by hostile, but highly inefficient and distracted, kings who were constantly suspected of Catholic leanings. The New England Puritans were back where they wanted to be: on the margins.

Meanwhile, as the first generation of Puritans died off and their children took their place, a persistent theme began to run through the Puritans' copious commentaries: we are not the men our fathers were. The very strenuousness of their literary forms—particularly their sermons on election days and a form of vitrolic preaching known as the jeremiad—testifies to their difficulty in maintaining the white–hot intensity of the founders. Poets such as Michael Wigglesworth, in his widely circulated "Day of Doom" and "God's Controversy with New England," saw droughts and other natural events as signs of God's punishment for Puritan backsliding. One imagines that there was a less dramatic, but probably more widespread, sense of melancholy over the limits of the Puritans' achievements, and the inevitable failure of their dream to meet up with reality.

This sense of gradual ebbing makes it difficult to say when the Puritan "moment," if that's what it was, actually ended. As late as the 1740s, amid the swirling eddies of religious revivals known as the First Great Awakening, ministers such as Jonathan Edwards sought to reinvigorate the Puritan tradition by calling on the faithful to embrace a tough–minded, but deeply satisfying, pursuit of spiritual rigor. (Edward's famous 1741 sermon "Sinners in the Hands of an Angry God," with its vivid images of God dangling worthless souls over a great furnace of wrath, contemplating whether to drop them in, is one of the great works of Puritan oratory.) But Edwards was dismissed by his congregation in 1750, an important signal of New England's exhaustion and impatience with the faith of its fathers.

Yet even figures whose work was premised on a rejection of a Puritan sensibility derived their energy from friction with it. The practical observations of Edwards's contemporary, the Boston-born Benjamin Franklin, were bracing precisely because they inverted, satirized, or reconfigured Puritan ideology. "So convenient a thing it is to be a *reasonable* creature, since it enables one to find or make a reason for everything one has a mind to do," the founder of *Poor Richard's Almanac* wrote in 1758. The line is simultaneously a subtle jab at the Puritan tendency to scrutinize (and rationalize) behavior, a sound (if glib) psychological principle, and, a (perhaps conscious) recognition of Franklin's own fall from Puritan grace. Once a form of comfort and/or preparation, and for a while staying the implacable hand of fate, health, wealth, and wisdom, had become a mere matter of social and physical hygiene to be pursued for its own sake. In so doing, it pointed toward a secularization of the American

Dream, and its evolution into forms we can recognize in our own day.

Franklin's life is also instructive for another reason: his youthful immigration to the thriving new city of (Quaker) Philadelphia in 1723 is indicative of the increasingly diverse range of possibilities, religious and otherwise, that characterized North America between the arrival of the Pilgrims and the advent of the American Revolution a century and a half later. The English weren't the only Protestants to colonize America; the Swedes and especially the Dutch gained a foothold in the mid–Atlantic until administrative control of their dominions was wrested from them by the English in the last quarter of the seventeenth century. German Mennonites and Quakers settled in eastern Pennsylvania. And with its teeming array of Indians, African immigrants (slave and free), and European traders—all speaking a variety of languages and worshiping in a variety of faiths—the Atlantic port of New Amsterdam/New York (which passed back and forth between the English and Dutch) was at least as much a melting pot in 1700 as it was 300 years later. Diversity has always been the norm.

This was true even within colonies that had always been solely under British control. Anglicans, Presbyterians, and Methodists had strongholds in a number of colonies even as they mingled among one another and jostled for converts. Though they were dominant in Massachusetts, the Puritans were always a minority in America at large (this may be one reason why they were so often combative and defensive). Moreover, the very success of their enterprise led to their dispersal; descendants of the first wave of Puritan settlement migrated westward in a steady stream that would ultimately reach the Pacific Northwest.

It so happens that English Catholics also had a colony of their own in British colonial America. This was Maryland, founded by the influential Calvert family. The mere fact of its existence is an important indication that far from receding into the distance, the Church was to find a place in America for the long haul even in largely hostile territory.

Actually, despite the creation of the Anglican Church, Roman Catholicism never wholly disappeared from England, and at different points in the 150 years following the break with Rome in 1534, the Church enjoyed measures of power and protection, particularly among the Stuart kings who reigned from 1610 to 1688. In 1632, George Calvert, also known as the First Baron Baltimore, induced Charles I to grant him land which had been part of the Virginia colony. Calvert, a convert to Catholicism, sought to establish a community where Catholics could worship without fear of persecution. He died before the charter for Maryland was granted, which then went to his son Cecilius Calvert, the Second Baron Baltimore. The settlement was established in 1634, a mere four years after the arrival of the Puritans in Massachusetts.

But English Catholics had a harder time taking root in America than the Puritans did. Much more than Massachusetts, Maryland was shaken by the events surrounding the English Civil War in the 1640s and 1650s. Lord Baltimore supported the king, while many Maryland colonists were sympathetic to the Puritan-controlled parliament. These differences led to a coup that drove Baltimore into exile in Virginia. He reasserted his authority in 1646, but it was increasingly apparent that the Puritans would win the civil war. To gain favor with the strongly anti-Catholic parliamentarians in the mother country and placate the Protestant majority in Maryland, the next Lord Baltimore appointed a non-Catholic as governor and named other Protestants to important positions in the government, eventually securing the cooperation and protection of Oliver Cromwell. At the same time he sought to ensure that the religious freedom of the Catholic minority would not be compromised by the Protestant majority. Largely as a result of his prodding, the legislature passed the Act Concerning Religion in 1649, assuring freedom of worship to all who believed in the Christian doctrine of the Trinity. It was a landmark piece of legislation in American history, but also somewhat defensive in character: Catholics championed tolerance because as a minority, they'd be wiped out if they didn't. The overthrow of the Stuart kings in the Glorious Revolution of 1688 led Protestant rebels to overthrow Maryland's government; the colony was placed under royal control in 1692. In the same year the Church of England was made the official church, and provisions for Catholic tolerance were repealed. For decades to come, it was difficult to be a practicing Catholic there or anywhere else in the British colonies.

In the broader sweep of Catholic history of the United States, the case of Maryland is significant in two ways, one of which would remain true to this day, and one which would not. The first is that insofar as Catholicism was permitted and flourished, it did so—and does so—on what might be termed a "Protestant" model, i.e., as one of a number of Christian faiths. It could not conquer America the way it had Europe a millennium before, and thus had to compete in a pluralistic religious landscape that was accepted at first because civil war was usually an unpalatable alternative, and later because religion ceased to be a thing Europeans were willing to fight over. Though we sometimes like to think of ourselves as "advanced" in commitment to diversity, religious tolerance has often been less a matter of principled conviction than indifference toward any kind of religion at all. When, for example, the British Empire implemented the Quebec Act of 1774, one provision of which made Roman Catholicism legal across the entire Atlantic seaboard, the move was widely viewed not as a matter of theological enlightenment, but as a painless means by which a secular British government could frighten its recalcitrant colonies with the prospect of political amalgamation with Canada.

The other notable aspect of the Maryland experience is the way in which it gave Catholicism an elite cast that would carry into— but not much beyond—the revolutionary era. The Calverts were rich and powerful founders, as were many of their co-religionists for some time to come. While this tendency engendered fear and envy, over the long term it served to legitimate Catholicism in much of American society, especially after the Revolution. (The epigraph that opens this chapter suggests both the lingering skepticism and subtle pull of Catholicism for Founding Father John Adams, whose mere presence in a Catholic church suggests how much had changed since the days his Puritan ancestors had founded Massachusetts.) Perhaps the best-known example of growing Catholic participation in American life is the life and work of Marylander John Carroll, who was elected to the Second Continental Congress in 1775 and was a signer of the Declaration of Independence. He later became the first American bishop in 1789. For much of the early national period, Catholicism was a small but generally accepted and even valued presence in national life.

This was not to last, however. Even before the advent of the Great Famine in Ireland, a growing stream of Catholic immigrants were decisively changing the face of the Church. The famine turned that stream into a flood, and the Irish diaspora of the 1840s and 1850s was augmented by the migration of refugees from Germany and Scandinavia around the same time. Later arrivals from southern and eastern Europe thoroughly transformed the nineteenth-century Church into a veritable Babel of language, ethnicity, and religious style. The organizational dominance of the Irish (for whom the clergy was an important form of social mobility for poor men and women) gave the Church cohesion, but their control was always subject to challenge by those, especially Germans, who pressured it to be more representative of American Catholicism as a whole.

The American church also developed a distinctively urban working-class orientation unlike any other Catholic Church in the world. In much of Europe and Latin America, the Church was widely considered an instrument of oppression, whether in its questionable alliances with corrupt regimes, or as a source of heavy taxation and social control in its own right. In the United States, by contrast, it was as often as not the ally of the labor union, the Democratic Party, and the immigrant aid society. If here too there was room for corruption, it was not typically a matter of betraying Catholics in the interests of the Protestant elite, or delivering them into the hands of Progressive reformers who usually came from that elite and assumed that "good government" would be defined on their terms.

There is some irony in all of this. Though the place of the Catholic Church has widely been viewed as somewhat uneasy in a democratic culture, many features of its American branch—its diversity, its receptivity to faithful men and women of talent, its intensely local and often political character—were broadly consonant with U.S. culture as a whole. One of the keenest observers of American society, the French aristocrat Alexis de Tocqueville, noted Catholicism's striking harmony with at least some aspects of American ideology in his classic study *Democracy in America*, published in two volumes in 1835 and 1840, just as the Catholic population in the United States was beginning to swell. Some remarks from the first volume are worth quoting in detail:

> I think that the Catholic religion has erroneously been regarded as the natural enemy of democracy. Among the various sects of Christians, Catholicism seems to me, on the contrary, to be one of the most favorable to equality of condition among men. In the Catholic Church the religious community is composed of only two elements: the priest and the people. The priest alone rises above the flank of his flock, and all below him are equal.
>
> On doctrinal points the Catholic faith places all human capacities on the same level; it subjects the wise and the ignorant, the man of genius and the vulgar crowd, to the details of the same creed; it imposes the same observances upon the rich and the needy; it inflicts the same austerities upon the strong and the weak; it listens to no compromise with mortal man, but, reducing all the human race to the same standard, it confounds all the distinctions of society at the foot of the same altar, even as they are confounded in the sight of God. If Catholicism predisposes the faithful to obedience, it certainly does not prepare them for inequality; but the contrary may be said of Protestantism, which generally tends to make men independent more than to render them equal. Catholicism is like an absolute monarchy; if the sovereign be removed, all the other classes of society are more equal than in republics.

"The men of our days are naturally little disposed to believe," Tocqueville wrote in a chapter on American Catholicism in the second volume of *Democracy in America*. "But as soon as they have any religion, they immediately find in themselves a latent instinct that urges them towards Catholicism."

Tocqueville, himself a Catholic, may have been indulging in some wishful thinking here. (He seemed to believe that Protestants would ultimately come to their senses and finally rejoin the One True Church.) On the contrary, it is abundantly clear that the sharp rise in the Catholic population provoked growing alarm and hostility on the part of native-born Protestants, even those in the South, where such immigrants were relatively rare. The so–called Know Nothing political party of the 1850s, for example, managed to unite a seriously divided pre-Civil War United States that could agree on little accept its hostility towards immigrants and Catholics (who were often one and the same).[3] After the Civil War, the Republican Party conflated Catholics and former Confederates alike as people of questionable loyalty and behavior, as the famous campaign slogan of 1884 decrying "Rum, Romanism, and Rebellion" suggests. As late as 1928, the Catholic faith of presidential candidate Al Smith was an issue, and while the mere fact of his candidacy suggests the ascent of Catholics in American national life, the whispering campaign that surrounded it and his decisive defeat suggested that old prejudices died hard.

By this point, discrimination against Catholics had been a fact of American life for three hundred years, far longer than the time (which, depending on your perspective, began some time in the last century) it has not been widespread and apparent. Even young Catholics today who cannot claim to have experienced anti–Catholic bias themselves are nevertheless aware that it was long a feature of American life, and one that put the national love and loyalty of their ancestors in question. Under such circumstances, one might well wonder what meaning or significance the American Dream might have had for those people—and Catholics were only one variety that included blacks, Jews, Asians, and even white Protestant women— who were explicitly excluded from recognition and participation in American life.

This is not an easy question to answer. One reason is that unlike the Puritans, many of those who came later to these shores were not impelled by carefully considered religious principles and self-conscious sacrifice, qualities that distinguished the Puritan American Dream. Instead, later arrivals were often desperate people for whom flight was a matter of simple survival, or a pragmatic act whose motives were so obvious that they rarely bothered to explicitly articulate them for themselves, let alone others. Nor, for those who lacked literacy, could they even if they desired.

One must also keep in mind that many Catholics viewed the

American Dream as largely irrelevant. We tend to forget how many immigrants—and their numbers, depending on the ethnic group or the period in question, were often very large—were in the United States temporarily. Those who remained were often deeply immersed in communities where their ethnic group, religion, and language were much more a part of everyday life than the ideology of the American Dream. Such an observation has particular relevance for the Catholic Church, which despite periodic attempts by some clerical leaders to participate more broadly in mainstream American life, devoted much of its time in the nineteenth century to building a self-contained culture of parochial churches, schools, and other institutions to shield its members from the hostility and temptations of the outside world.

Finally, even when paternalistic priests or small-minded bigots could not limit Catholic access and participation in American society, it often took two or even three generations before a Catholic would seriously explore what progressive reformer Herbert Croly called "the promise of American life" in his 1915 book of the same name. Moreover, those who *were* willing and able to engage with the American Dream were not always in a position to respond in clear ways that would speak to future generations. It is not really until the twentieth century that one can begin to discern an intellectual infrastructure of artists, writers, philosophers, and others who communicated with themselves, the Catholic lay community, and American culture at large in ways that bound them all together.

All this said, there is little question that the American Dream has nevertheless long been a fixture of the Catholic imagination. Actually, it would be more accurate to speak of Catholic imaginations, plural, because as within any social subgroup, no two individuals respond in quite the same way. And yet it is possible, nevertheless, to speak of a series of varied responses rooted in a shared historical experience. Without presuming to be definitive, we can perhaps use the context sketched here to explore a few such responses in some of the better-known Catholic cultural documents of our time, and in so doing gain a better grasp of where we've been and earn a rich sense of the possibilities as to where we might yet go.

PART II

EMBODYING THE DREAM
AMERICAN CATHOLIC ARCHETYPES

DISTANT VIEW

F. Scott Fitzgerald in 1937, in a photo by Carl Van Vechten. *(Photo from the Van Vechten Collection of the Library of Congress)*

Chapter Three

FATAL ATTRACTION:
THE CASE OF JAY GATSBY

*I am ashamed to say that my Catholicism is scarcely more
than a memory—no, that's wrong, it's more than that; at
any rate I go not to the church nor mumble stray nothings
over crystalline beads.*

—F. Scott Fitzgerald, in a letter to Edmund Wilson,
August 15, 1919

When F. Scott Fitzgerald was born on September 24, 1896, the
American Catholic Church was in the midst of a long and at
times bitter debate about its identity. On one side of the divide were
the so-called Americanists, one of whose leaders, John Ireland, was
the bishop of Fitzgerald's native St. Paul. Ireland and his allies
believed that the Church—whose membership quadrupled from three
million in 1860 to twelve million in 1900, making it the nation's
largest religious denomination—had attained critical mass in the
United States, and could now engage with institutions like public
schools and labor unions in productive ways without compromising
its fundamental identity. Critics of this view, sometimes called *Romani*
for their orientation toward the Vatican, were mindful of the hostility the Church had long received, and believed its strength lay in
maintaining a separate identity and separate institutions, like parochial schools, as clear alternatives to the seductions of secular
American life. Amid a series of crosscurrents, scandals, and shifting
alliances, Pope Leo XIII finally weighed in with a letter, *Testem
Benevolentiae*, which pronounced that "We cannot approve the opinions which some comprise under the head of Americanism." There
was perhaps less to this assertion than meets the eye; as historian

Charles Morris has explained, Leo's definition of Americanism involved "a series of esoteric doctrines few Americans would have recognized" as such. Moreover, Morris argues, "the grand Catholic compromise" that emerged from the controversy rendered unto America what was America's in terms of national love and loyalty even as it affirmed the primacy of parochial schools and other instruments of Catholic identity. Still, the overall cast of the Church hierarchy was separatist and conservative, and would remain so for decades to come.

The same cannot necessarily be said for Catholic laity. Over the course of the twentieth century, Catholics increasingly gained access to the American Dream—graduating from colleges, buying houses, owning businesses—and for many of them the double consciousness inherent in U.S. Catholicism only became more pressing. Not only did many of the premises of American life, such as secular achievement and individualism, run counter to those of traditional Catholicism, but many American Catholics felt able, even forced, to choose between God and country. Indeed, the very notion of an identity as something you *choose* is itself characteristically American. And while it is impossible to calculate just how these dilemmas played themselves out, in part because many avoided choosing or concluded it was impossible to choose, it's unmistakably clear that many Americans placed a great deal of faith in the American Dream.

The life and work of F. Scott Fitzgerald is emblematic of this distinctively modern American Catholic double consciousness. The first Catholic novelist to make a deep and lasting impact in the culture at large, Fitzgerald's stance toward the American Dream—a striking combination of fascination and skepticism—is notable for both its clarity and the way it continues to represent the feelings of many Americans on the subject. Fitzgerald's perspective drew on widespread Catholic currents that were all the more powerful for their subtle, even unconscious qualities. These currents both reflected and influenced the world in which he lived—a world which, in many respects, is our world as well.

Fitzgerald's family is steeped in American history. His paternal ancestors arrived with the first batch of Catholic settlers in Maryland in 1634 and were prominent, if at times embattled, plantation owners straight through the Revolution. And as no Fitzgerald biographer fails to note, he was distantly related to his namesake, Francis Scott Key, author of the national anthem. Another relative, Mary Surratt, was (probably wrongly) executed for her role in harboring the conspirators of Abraham Lincoln's assassination; in adulthood, Fitzgerald's parents pestered him to write a book exonerating her. Few figures then or since could claim such a colorful pedigree.

Fitzgerald's father, Edward, was born in Rockville County, Maryland, in 1853. He went west to make his fortune, and spent time in Chicago before settling in St. Paul, Minnesota, to become president of a furniture manufacturing company. That's probably where he met Fitzgerald's mother, Mollie McQuillan, who he married in 1890.

In contrast the to the Fitzgeralds, the McQuillan story is part of a very different American saga: the Irish diaspora. In 1843 a nine-year-old boy, Philip Francis McQuillan (or "P.F.," as he was known) emigrated from Ireland and settled in Galena, Illinois. In 1857 he moved to St. Paul and started a multimillion-dollar clothing business. A contributor to the construction of the city's St. Mary's Church in 1866, he also served on the board of trustees for its Home for Friendless Girls. He died at forty-three in 1877, leaving behind a widow and five children. Mollie, the oldest, was convent-educated, and accompanied her mother and siblings to Europe four times, growing up as part of a respectable, though not quite leading, family in the St. Paul Catholic community where Swedes still had more stature than the Irish.

Mollie married Ted Fitzgerald when she was twenty-nine and approaching spinsterhood. By the time their only son was born six years later, the couple, who shuttled back and forth between upstate New York and St. Paul, had endured a number of setbacks, among them severe financial losses and the deaths of two daughters (Scott would have a surviving younger sister). A sense of receded fortunes pervades characterizations of the future novelist's family history, both those written by himself and later biographers.

Fitzgerald's parents were both practicing Catholics, though his mother was probably more devout. They sent him to parochial schools, notably Newman Academy, a boarding school in Hackensack, New Jersey. While there he befriended Father Cyril Sigourney Webster Fay, a Newman trustee with strong connections to the powerful Cardinal James Gibbons of Baltimore, who had been a savvy conciliator in the Americanist debate of the 1880s and 1890s. Fay, an Episcopalian convert who was ultimately appointed monsignor by Pope Benedict XV, was one of the more important figures in Fitzgerald's life, an intellectually minded aesthete who nurtured the boy's literary ambitions. As Fitzgerald later explained, Fay and another converted Catholic mentor, the Anglo-Celtic writer and lecturer Shane Leslie, made Catholicism seem "a dazzling, golden thing, dispelling its oppressive mugginess and giving the succession of days upon days, passing under its plaintive ritual, the romantic glamour of an adolescent dream." Fay's death in 1919, while Fitzgerald was at Princeton, was a deeply felt loss.

Of course, having Catholic parents, attending Catholic schools, and being able to say that some of your best friends were Catholics (another priest, Father Joseph Barron of St. Paul, was the godfather of Fitzgerald's daughter Scottie), does not necessarily mean that one is religious. Indeed, there is much evidence that the young Fitzgerald regarded his religion in a manner that was callow at best. "Why I can go up to New York on a terrible party and then come back into the church and pray—and mean every word of it, too!" he told Princeton classmate and future literary critic Edmund Wilson.

In any event, Fitzgerald's primary preoccupations at Princeton alternated between one "terrible party" after another and intensive writing for school publications and dramatic productions (he seemed to regard his courses as a distraction, and left Princeton without receiving a degree). He enlisted in the First World War during his senior year in 1917, and was stationed on an army base in Alabama, where he met his future wife, Zelda Sayre, the wild daughter of a justice on the state's supreme court. Despite the consternation with which their whirlwind romance was met, and doubts he could actually support her, the two were married in 1920.

Fitzgerald seemed to regard his religious background as something to be outgrown. An oft-quoted notebook entry summarizing 1917–1918 described the period as his "last year as a Catholic," and a 1925 visit to Rome led him to describe the pro-fascist Pope Pius XI and his entourage as "Pope Siphilus the Sixth and His Morons." Even the decision to attend Princeton—a decidedly Protestant school founded by Presbyterians—suggests other priorities, as does his rather unceremonious wedding ceremony with Zelda Sayre, an Episcopalian (he didn't bother to hold a reception). For much of their marriage the couple seemed far more dedicated to hedonism than spirituality, and while Zelda apparently became more religious at the end of her life as she struggled with clinical depression, Fitzgerald clung more tightly to alcohol than any otherworldly commitment. When he died, all too prematurely, in 1940, the Baltimore diocese where he wished to be interred refused to allow burial in a Catholic cemetery (though his wish was finally granted in 1975 when his and his wife's remains were joined with those of his father in a cemetery in suburban Washington, D.C.).

Of course, one of the main places one should look for a spiritual presence in Fitzgerald's life is his writing, and here it appears a real, if limited, degree of engagement that ebbed sharply as he matured. As befits an embryonic writer with a double consciousness, he received his first recognition when he was ten years old for an essay on George Washington and Ignatius Loyola. Two of his early stories, "Benediction" and "The Last Ordeal," have seminary settings and focus on characters who struggle with their religious identities. The Catholicism of the protagonist of his first novel, *This Side of Paradise*, is a defining element of his personality, and his friendship with a character named Monsignor Darcy—one modeled closely on his mentor Fay, to whom Fitzgerald dedicated the book—is crucial in the transformation of an immature "personality" into a substantial "personage." Yet explicitly religious figures and themes were relatively rare in Fitzgerald's subsequent work. In 1955, when the novelist's reputation was at the beginning of a sharp ascent from a literary curio to literary giant, Leslie Fiedler, one of the most important American literary critics of the twentieth century, argued that Catholicism was not a major element in Fitzgerald's fiction. "His books have no religious insights, only religious decór," Fiedler asserted. Conceding that images and metaphors occasionally crept into Fitzgerald's work—such as the ruined psychologist making a gesture reminiscent of a "papal cross" at the end of his 1934 novel *Tender Is the Night*—Fiedler nevertheless maintained that "there is in Fitzgerald no profound sense of evil or sin, only of guilt; and no gods except the Rich."

A quarter-century later, biographer Matthew Bruccoli, a scholar who has bibliographically sifted Fitzgerald's oeuvre more than any other, agreed. "Despite the generalization that no Irishman ever really leaves Holy Mother Church, Fitzgerald left without a backward glance or lingering guilt," Bruccoli wrote in 1981. "His spells of devoutness had come when his imagination was stimulated by some religious role or some priest. Fitzgerald's Catholicism died with Fay. Zelda replaced the influence of Fay and the Church."

These are plausible assertions. But they tend to underestimate the degree to which an American Catholic sensibility can shape a cultural vision in ways that do not necessarily have obvious religious sources. If one is willing to think more broadly of sacred influences on secular subjects, then Fitzgerald's most famous novel, a book with virtually no specifically Catholic references, might nevertheless be seen as a distinctively Catholic book.

✻　✻　✻

> I am half black Irish and half old American stock with the usual exaggerated ancestral pretensions. The black Irish half of the family had the money and looked down upon the Maryland side of the family who had, and really had, that certain series of reticences and obligations that go under the poor old shattered word "breeding" (modern form "inhibitions"). So being born in that atmosphere of crack, wise crack and countercrack I developed a two cylinder inferiority complex. So if I were elected King of Scotland tomorrow after graduating from Eton, Magdelene and the Guards with an embryonic history that tied me to the Plantagonets [Plantagenets, an early dynasty of English kings], I would still be a *parvenue*.

> —*F. Scott Fitzgerald in a letter to fellow novelist John O'Hara, 1933*

Nowadays, an artistically minded young person typically aspires to be a film director or pop musician. But not that long ago, the characteristic ambition of such a person would be to write "the great American novel." "Great American novel" is a kind of generic phrase—and a kind of generic American Dream. The implicit assumption was that the person who actually wrote such a book would be from a relatively modest background but whose talent was so evident that he (and this was long enough ago that one could speak of "he" unselfconsciously) would be able to make the world pay notice.

Much in the way one might talk about sports legends or important presidents, it still sometimes works as a conversational gambit to ask a group of book lovers to name the quintessential great American novel. *The Adventures of Huckleberry Finn? The Grapes of Wrath?* Maybe *Catcher in the Rye?* They're all good candidates. But high on any list—I'm willing to bet at the top of most lists, and the kind of book someone who preferred another would somehow have to displace—is *The Great Gatsby.* Part of the reason, no doubt, is F. Scott Fitzgerald's image as a romantic figure whose talent brought his fame and riches in the Jazz Age, a phrase Fitzgerald coined (despite almost complete ignorance of what jazz was all about). Yet generation after generation of readers have found something fresh and relevant about the book. Indeed, much of its appeal is the way it still seems to describe a modern world that, despite all the technological and social changes since, still seems recognizably ours, from its suburban lawns to its hard–boiled irony about consumer culture.

It is thus notable that the novel, while not an abject critical or commercial failure, was not especially cherished in Fitzgerald's lifetime. He was grievously disappointed that it only sold about twenty thousand copies by the time of his death, and that plenty of negative reviews were sprinkled in among some very good, even prophetic, ones. Since the 1950s, however, the book has only grown in popularity, having been translated into thirty-five languages and selling more copies each month than were sold in Fitzgerald's entire lifetime. By that standard, millions of readers have come to know the novel from fairly early on in life; it has become part of that rare stratum of work that can be described as part of a shared national culture.

But what, if anything, makes *The Great Gatsby* great? The answers, naturally, vary and include those of reluctant readers forced to trudge through it in high school English and who perhaps as a result find nothing great about it at all. (Part of my goal here is to generate a few second looks, along with some first ones.) Of those who do respond positively to the book, many no doubt regard it as a powerful love story. Clearly, it is. But it's also more, and to explain at least one more way how, it might be useful here to review the plot, in a concise way that the book deliberately delivers in bits and pieces:

James Gatz (or Jimmy, as his father calls him) is born in 1890 in North Dakota. After attending St. Olaf's College in southern Minnesota for two weeks, the seventeen-year-old boy drifts to Lake Superior, where he works digging clams, fishing for salmon, and other odd jobs. While there, Gatz meets Dan Cody, a millionaire copper magnate who hires him to serve as a steward-mate-skipper for his yacht. For the next five years, Gatz sails the world with Cody, who adopts the boy as a protégé, and trusts him to keep tabs on him when he drinks too much. When Cody dies in 1912, he leaves Gatz $25,000, but Gatz never receives the money because of the machinations of Cody's mistress, a newspaperwoman. What he does inherit, however, is a sense of worldliness and style he will use to dramatic effect in years to come with the new name and identity he invents for himself.

Gatz's whereabouts are unknown between 1912 and 1917, at which point he appears in Louisville, Kentucky, as a lieutenant in the United States Army awaiting transport to France to fight in the First World War. Here, he falls in love with the beautiful young Daisy Fay, whose background is far more distinguished than his own. Visiting her house with other officers from his local army base, and then alone, brings his life into vivid clarity: she will be the love of his life. But Daisy, while returning his attentions, is out of reach. This is not only because he is about to go to war but also because his lowly origins make his very presence in the house a "colossal accident." Nevertheless, he is determined to win her.

After being decorated for distinguished service in the war and a stint at Oxford, he returns to make his fortune via shadowy means (apparently he has something to do with the notorious Black Sox Scandal of 1919, in which the Chicago White Sox allegedly colluded with bookmakers to intentionally lose the World Series). Meanwhile, Daisy Fay comes out as a debutante and marries Tom Buchanan, a Yale graduate from a respectable family. Daisy bears a daughter, and the young family moves from Santa Barbara to Chicago, finally settling on a waterfront estate on Long Island.

How do we know all of this? We learn most of it second hand from the book's narrator, Nick Carraway who himself learns it second hand. Nick, a fellow Midwesterner, is Daisy's second cousin once removed (the fact that they're related, but distantly, is suggestive of their characters) and knew her husband Tom at Yale. Nick arrives in New York in the spring of 1922 to become a bond trader, and rents a small house on a peninsula across the bay from Daisy and Tom. It soon emerges that Nick's rich next-door neighbor, who throws wild parties at his baronial estate and who is the source of endless gossip, is Daisy's old suitor, who now goes by the name of Jay Gatsby—or just "Gatsby" to those who enjoy his parties and speculate on his background (is he a bootlegger? Did he kill a man?). Those parties, as it turns out, have a determined purpose: to lure Daisy. And Nick, as it turns out, becomes the agent of their reunion, and the man who bears witness to the ensuing tragedy.

Virtually all students of *The Great Gatsby* are struck by Fitzgerald's decision to narrate the story from Nick's point of view, a choice that gives the book any number of distinctive qualities. What I want to emphasize here is that Nick is figuratively (and almost surely literally) a Protestant character. His last name, Carraway, has a straightforward Anglo-Saxon simplicity that indicates his ethnic background. His Yale degree—a place he describes with a notable sense of unself-conscious ease—also suggests as much. Even the measured (and faintly condescending) tone of his father, who Nick reports in the beginning of the novel has told him not to criticize those who have not had the advantages Nick has and who allocates a measured string of financial support to allow his son to achieve self-sufficiency in New York, is redolent of a Protestant work ethic and related values (like thrift). Nick is the closest thing we have to an objective observer in the novel, and to a very great extent he can function in this role precisely because he is a quintessential middle American, far more so than even other presumably Protestant characters, like Tom and Daisy Buchanan, whose sense of dissipation has left them unmoored not only from any code of religious or ethical values, but also from the middle America from which they also came.

And Gatsby? Is he the "Catholic" figure? Basically, yes. But one can't be entirely certain: there are some hints, for example, that Gatsby[4] is Jewish. I say so partly because his close associate is Meyer Wolfsheim (a character modeled on the Jewish gangster Arnold Rothstein, one of the principal figures in the Black Sox Scandal of 1919), and partly because Gatsby's family name, Gatz, is evocative of the kind of truncated Eastern European name shortened by immigration officials who couldn't pronounce the multisyllabic Yiddish, Slavic, and other languages that accompanied new arrivals from that part of the world, a great many of whom were Jewish.[5] On the other hand, Gatsby's first name, James, one of the twelve apostles, is *not* a standard Jewish name.[6] In these respects, as in others, he remains an enigmatic figure.

In a sense, you might say that it doesn't matter whether Gatsby was born Catholic, Jewish, or for that matter, Hindu. The important thing is that he's an outsider lacking an understanding of the subtle social cues that structure WASP life. In fact, Jews, who tended to be newer arrivals than many Catholics, were actually more marginal in American life at the time and long after, which may be one good reason for thinking of Gatsby as Jewish: it dramatizes even more the way mere money can never wholly confer status in any society, a lesson Gatsby fails to learn. (Were the novel written today, Gatsby might well be a Colombian immigrant rumored to be a drug dealer.) To repeat the point I made at the start of this book, a sense of double consciousness characterizes many subcultures in American life, and given our long history of inviting invidious distinctions, it is well worth emphasizing those experiences that are widely shared— especially the experience of being an outsider—in our different racial and ethnic contexts.

Nevertheless, there are good reasons to think of Gatsby as a

Catholic figure. One reason concerns an episode Fitzgerald decided not to include in the book but which became a separate short story: "Absolution," a story about an eleven-year-old boy and priest, which appeared in a literary magazine, *The American Mercury*, in 1924. Ten years later, Fitzgerald explained to a critic that the story "was intended to be a picture of [Gatsby's] early life, but that I cut it because I preferred to preserve a sense of mystery." It would probably be a mistake to insist a direct correlation between the boy of "Absolution" and Gatsby; not only do they have different names, but their fathers have different personalities. Moreover, other Fitzgerald novels changed greatly in the course of their development; *Tender Is the Night*, for example, was originally conceived as a story about a man who kills his mother. There is nevertheless an unmistakable affinity between the boy of the "Absolution" and the man of *The Great Gatsby*.

The focus of "Absolution" is handsome, precocious Rudolph Miller, who goes into a confessional and recites his sins to a priest, Adolphus Schwartz, whose interest in childish romantic escapades borders on prurience. Still, the sacrament proceeds in a fairly routine fashion (with ordinary sins like "being mean to an old lady" jostling with more distinctive ones like "not believing I was the son of my parents") until the priest unexpectedly asks the boy, "Have you told any lies?" Rudolph impulsively answers, "Oh no, Father, I never tell lies"—which is, of course, a lie. He leaves the confessional without revealing this fact, and to escape the danger of receiving communion while in a state of sin the next morning, concocts a plan to "accidentally" drink water before Mass and thus be ineligible to receive communion. Unfortunately, the boy's suspicious, frustrated father comes into the kitchen at precisely the wrong moment and angrily rebukes him for drinking the water, ordering him to go to confession before church services begin that morning. But "a wild, proud anger" rises in Rudolph, and while he obeys his father's command, he no longer feels compelled to respect the spirit of paternal authority, sacred or secular. Father Schwartz is again his confessor, and Rudolph flatly owns up to missing morning prayers—once again remaining silent about his lying. He usually feels ashamed when he lacks money to put in the collection plate because he wants to impress a local girl in the parish, but this time he views the procedure with clinical detachment. And disregarding his earlier fears, he goes ahead and receives communion. From now on, he will live in the world of his alter ego, "Blatchford Sarnemington," a suave, confident dandy who never feels self-doubt or suffers petty humiliations.

And yet the transformation is not quite complete. Walking back to his pew after receiving communion, Rudolph hears "the sharp tap of cloven hoofs were upon the floor, and he knew that it was a dark poison he carried inside his heart." Moreover, the story ends with him back in confession with Father Schwartz, whose grip on piety is as wobbly as the boy's is on apostasy. When the priest explains that "When a lot of people get together in the best places things go glimmering," even Rudolph recognizes that the man is insane. And yet he acknowledges the inchoate feelings Father Schwartz describes in his almost incoherent babble about parties, lights, and amusement parks. "All this talking seemed particularly strange and awful to Rudolph, because this man was a priest," he thinks. "He sat there, half terrified, his beautiful eyes wide open and staring at Father Schwartz. But beneath his terror he felt his convictions were confirmed. There was something ineffably gorgeous somewhere that had nothing to do with God." The priest then suffers an apparent a heart attack, while outside, in the world to which Rudolph will return with new conviction, full-blooded blond-haired girls are luring farm boys to lie with them beside wheat fields. Rudolph may have left the Church, but its residue seems to give life a special glow.

The similarities between Rudolph Miller and James Gatz are obvious and striking: both come from undistinguished Midwestern backgrounds toward which they feel alienated, even ashamed; both have ineffectual fathers who don't understand them; both project romantic feelings onto beautiful girls (and feel that money is necessary to impress them); and most obvious of all, both invent personas to house new conceptions of themselves. One can well imagine Rudolph Miller dispensing with the sophomoric, almost unpronounceable alias of Blatchford Sarnemington in favor of the less awkward and more romantic Jay Gatsby, fully embracing the glimmering, worldly world.

It's the peculiar quality of that glimmering world that gives *The Great Gatsby* one of its more subtle, but important, Catholic dimensions. All in all, "Absolution" seems to be a fairly damning indictment of the Church, one that depicts it as repressive, hypocritical, and largely irrelevant to an ordinary child, let alone one with the beauty and sensitivity of Rudolph. So it is not surprising that Fitzgerald, whose own religious engagement had sharply ebbed, might choose to sever *The Great Gatsby*—a story whose concerns were rooted in his adulthood as surely as "Absolution" was in his childhood—from any obvious religious moorings (one can't help but wonder about Fitzgerald giving superficially beautiful Daisy Fay the same last name as his real-life mentor). Nevertheless, there's a romantic, almost baroque quality to Fitzgerald's own prose that suggests a sensuousness characteristic of Catholic art and ritual.

Take, for example, this description of Daisy's house in Louisville, which Gatsby had visited while stationed there before the war:

> It amazed him. He had never been in such a beautiful house before. But what gave it an air of breathless intensity was that Daisy lived there—it was as casual a thing to her as his tent out at the camp was to him. There was an air of ripe mystery about it, a hint of bedrooms upstairs more beautiful and cool than other bedrooms, of gay and radiant activities taking place through its corridors and of romances that were not musty and laid away already in lavender but fresh and breathing and redolent of this year's shining motor cars and of dances whose flowers were scarcely withered. It excited him too that many men had already loved Daisy—it increased her value in his eyes. He felt their presence all about the house, pervading the air with the shades and echoes of still vibrant emotions.

For Gatsby, Daisy's home, is a cathedral, a house of many mansions. "Breathless intensity," "ripe mystery," allusions to the scent of fresh flowers and the now-gone but lingering souls who have worshipped at the shrine of the immaculate Daisy: all suggest an idealized vision of the Church, albeit one refracted—and distorted—through the all-too-perishable Daisy (who, when he kissed her for the first time, "blossomed like a flower and the incarnation was complete"). Gatsby's baroque house and car bespeak a penchant for ornamentation (some might say gaudiness) typical of Catholic tastes, and his weekly parties represent a kind of inverted parody of Mass. Insofar as there is something ineffably gorgeous here—and even Nick, our stolid voice of reason, cannot help but finally believe "there was something gorgeous" about Gatsby—it's far from clear that it has nothing to do with God, a God who, perhaps despite Fitzgerald's growing distance from the Church, continues to have recognizably Catholic features.

And that God, it increasingly becomes clear, is a force to be reckoned with on the road to the American Dream.

✻   ✻   ✻

I guess I am too much a moralist at heart and really want to preach at people in some acceptable form rather than to entertain them.

—*Fitzgerald in a letter to his daughter,*
November 1939

One need not be an especially acute reader to know from the outset that Gatsby's quest for Daisy is not promising. We meet her even before we meet him, and so we see how shallow she is, and most of us know from experience that such strong desire is an unstable compound. Any plausible hopes we might have for Gatsby's dream of Daisy evaporate when Nick advises him not to "ask too much of her" because "you can't repeat the past." To which Gatsby responds: "Can't repeat the past? Why of course you can!" Subsequent events in the novel reveal just how disastrous it is to attempt to railroad through the hard realities, like time, space, and the fickleness of the human heart, that mortal life imposes.

But the skepticism that *The Great Gatsby* engenders about its protagonist's American Dream is not only a matter of its fable-like plot of a man who pursues unseemly ends through unseemly means and pays for his dream with his life. Fitzgerald also gives the reader other cues, the most important of which is the famous image of the so-called valley of ashes, presided over by an optometrist's advertisement featuring the enormous eyes of Doctor T. J. Eckleburg. This haunting image, which opens the second chapter of the novel and is the setting for its climax, has sometimes been interpreted as a kind of modernist metaphor for the wasteland of humanity in a godless age (indeed, the name T. J. Eckleburg is reputedly a reference to T. S. Eliot, author of "The Waste Land," who himself felt the pull of Catholicism, particularly at the end of his life). There's a mute quality to Eckleburg and the valley of ashes that make them all the more unnerving, but at the same time a notion of divine judgment is not wholly absent. When the distraught, cuckolded husband and widower George Wilson tells his neighbor that he had told his wife, "You can fool me but you can't fool God!" Wilson's neighbor, who had counseled him to seek out a priest, is disturbed to realize that Wilson is addressing his words directly at Dr. Eckleburg. When Wilson goes on to say that "God sees everything," his neighbor replies "that's just an advertisement"—a pronouncement that some readers might be forgiven for thinking otherwise, and one that suggests the degree to which the newer god of industrial capitalism has still not quite conquered its rivals.

But not all of Fitzgerald's commentary is redolent of a distant deity whose presence, insofar as it is discernible at all, has a distinctly Old Testament quality of implacable judgment. There are unmistakable allusions to Gatsby as a Christ-like figure as the novel approaches its climax: he's a man who dies for someone else's sins, at three in the afternoon, and whose true identity is revealed three days later by his father. It is, of course, highly ironic that this pathetic fraud of a man, an unregenerate sinner, would be the redeeming figure in the novel. But that's also what makes it all the more appropriate and satisfying.

There's also a mystical strain that runs through the book. It's apparent when Gatsby feels his dream is almost within his grasp, and a moment when Nick makes some deeply suggestive remarks:

> Through all he said, even through his appalling sentimentality, I was reminded of something—an elusive rhythm, a

fragment of lost words, that I had heard somewhere a long time ago. For a moment a phrase tried to take shape in my mouth and my lips parted like a dumb man's, as though there was more struggling upon them than a wisp of startled air. But they made no sound and what I had almost remembered was uncommunicable forever.

The problem with the American Dream, this passage implicitly suggests, is not exactly that it's corrupt or vain. Indeed, the great paradox of *The Great Gatsby* is that even as Gatsby pursues his dream through instruments of fraud and adultery there is a deeply compelling purity about his ambition, especially given the smug pieties of those around him (hence Nick's sincere pronouncement that Gatsby is "worth the whole damn bunch of them put together"). Rather, the real problem is that any secular dream is finally too incomplete a vessel to contain longings that elude human expression or comprehension. That's why we have religion.

Still we—and by "we" I mean everyone, the world over for all time—go on dreaming. Even those of us who have the means and desire to pursue their dreams finally have no power over what they happen to be: dreams usually come to us unbidden, and typically are not practical or easy to achieve (otherwise they wouldn't be dreams). What makes the *American* Dream American is not that our dreams are any better, worse, or more interesting than anyone else's, but that we happen to live in a country constituted of dreams, whose very justification continues to rest on it being a place where one can pursue distant goals. This is something Fitzgerald understood very well. "Gatsby believed in the green light, the orgastic future that year by year recedes before us," he writes in the soaring conclusion of the novel, whose vision zooms out to encompass the whole of American history all the way back to Dutch sailors who encountered a new world "commensurate with [their] capacity to wonder." Yet, he concludes, such visions are finally a mirage that leads us to think we're moving toward our goals when instead we're moving away from them: "So we beat on, boats against the current, borne ceaselessly into the past."

The American Dream, F. Scott Fitzgerald is telling us, is a

fatally attractive thing. What makes this message so powerful is the deep sense of engagement and sympathy he feels toward Gatsby even as he demonstrates, with the help of the relatively detached Nick, how squalid Gatsby really is. These qualities of engagement, sympathy, and detachment—and that leveling instinct de Tocqueville referred to in *Democracy in America* as distinctive of American Catholics—are products of Fitzgerald's double consciousness: he understands both the bright possibilities of American life and the restrictions Catholicism imposes. And vice-versa, for Catholicism is not without its brightness, and American life also has its limits (as suggested by Nick himself, who for all his wisdom is nevertheless tempted by the life he finds in Gatsby's world, but ultimately retreats back to the safety of the Midwest). Fitzgerald's religion, as it turns out, was more than a memory or recitations on crystalline beads; it was an indispensable ingredient in the creation of his greatest work. And it would remain so, down through his long, fitful decline, harrowingly chronicled in the series of highly confessional letters, essays, and notes that were posthumously collected and published as *The Crack-Up* (1945).

But Fitzgerald's Catholicism was finally a particular *kind* of Catholicism. To a great extent, it was bound up in ethnicity: by birth and the vicissitudes of their dominance of American church machinery, he imbibed the puritanically tinged, pessimistic strand *Irish* Catholicism that managed to survive, even thrive, in an increasingly secular land of hope. "The point of being Irish is knowing that the world will break your heart," goes an old saying. In life and art, Fitzgerald seemed determined to reaffirm this belief in an American context.

It's important to note, however, that Fitzgerald's "cheap Irish love of defeat," as a dismissive Ernest Hemingway once termed it, was not necessarily cheap or Irish. A whole tradition of gangster movies, for example—one that runs from the Howard Hawks version of *Scarface* (1932), with its Italian American protagonist, to the Brian DePalma version of *Scarface* (1983) with its Cuban immigrant protagonist, and beyond—depict characters who pursue and attain an (inherently?) warped American Dream, only to be inevitably destroyed, less by external forces than the fallen nature of their own characters. For all his undeniable originality, Fitzgerald didn't invent this perspective on the American Dream, and it's the fact that it was, and is, widely shared that finally makes it so important.

But is this perspective right? *Should* one view the American Dream as a fatal compromise? Lacking any source of scientific proof, this is something that each individual has to decide for oneself. It's worth pointing out, however, that such a stance is not without its risks, not only in terms of potentially casting a pall over a person's life—the mere question "Why bother?" has a depressing effect built into it—but also in stunting any number of worthwhile dreams. Slavery, for example, might never have been abolished had those who embarked on this quest concluded, as many reasonable people, far too many of them Catholic, did at the time, that it was too complicated or unrealistic to pursue. To be sure, the African American dream of freedom has turned out to be less of a panacea than many of its greatest champions (many, though not all, of them white Protestants) and beneficiaries (many, though not all, of them black Protestants) hoped, but that doesn't necessarily mean the American Dream is nothing more than a mirage. Perhaps this is simply a way of illustrating that imperfect outcomes are better than perfect goals— something Gatsby refused to accept—or that collective dreams are finally more worthwhile than individual ones—something Fitzgerald, unlike some of his contemporaries, never seriously explored. In the end, the validity of the American Dream, spiritually and otherwise, may really depend on the Dream, which, of course, comes in many shapes and sizes.

American Catholicism also comes in many shapes and sizes. One can begin to appreciate just how unique, as well as resonant, Fitzgerald's version was when it is juxtaposed against some others, notably that of a writer who created a heroine who proved to be even more famous than Jay Gatsby. Perhaps it was just a coincidence the woman who gave us Scarlett O'Hara happened to be born Catholic. Then again, it may have mattered far more than she, or many other readers, have realized.

CROSSING DIXIE

Margaret Mitchell holding a copy of her hugely successful novel in 1938. Though she decisively rejected her faith after her mother's death in 1919, the Catholicism of her protagonist, Scarlett O'Hara, is notable for its subtle—and surprisingly powerful—impact in *Gone with the Wind*. *(Photo by William Warnecke from the New York World-Telegram & Sun Collection, Library of Congress)*

Chapter Four

INCOMPLETE DENIAL:
THE CASE OF SCARLETT O'HARA

[Scarlett O'Hara] obeyed her mother and going to her room gabbled a hasty rosary. When she rose from her knees she did not feel as comforted as she had formerly felt after prayer. For some time she had felt that God was not watching out for her, the Confederates or the South, in spite of the millions of prayers ascending to Him daily.

—Margaret Mitchell, *Gone with the Wind*

*G*one with the Wind? A *Catholic* story? Not really. Actually, when most people think of *GWTW* (as those in the know refer to it, and as I will henceforth refer to it here), they picture a 1939 movie, not a 1936 book, and that movie is typically considered a romance between the headstrong Scarlett O'Hara and the dashing Rhett Butler (Vivian Leigh and Clark Gable). Others view *GWTW* as a Civil War story; indeed, even now the version of the war in the movie influences popular perceptions to a degree to which academic historians never have. And although it might not be the first thing that comes to mind, most of us would probably concede that *GWTW* is also a story about the (temporarily Confederate) American Dream: a tale about a child of immigrants struggling to extend a legacy; a fable about not getting what you want, and not appreciating what you have; even a subtle affirmation of the most important American Dream: home ownership—in this case, Tara, the O'Hara plantation that is the only recipient of faithful love in Scarlett's life. But Catholicism? Hard to figure that one.

One reason it's hard to see is that the film version of *GWTW* necessarily streamlined much of the story. As long as the four-hours-plus movie is, it only covers a fraction of the material covered in the thousand-page-plus book. Characters, plot lines, and settings had to be cut. But there were more than such logistical consider-ations at stake. Margaret Mitchell's book is a highly detailed portrait of a very specific Southern world, and producer David O. Selznick wanted a compelling, but not distracting, portrait that would be appealing and comprehensible to a global audience. That meant sim-plifying otherwise confusing details. There was also the matter of censorship. Even if Selznick had wanted to retain some of the Catholic aspects of Mitchell's book, he almost certainly would not have been allowed to. The Catholic–dominated Production Code Office under the administration of the powerful Joseph Breen would never have permitted the discussion of abortion, for example, that takes place in the book.

Another reason why the Catholic dimension of *GWTW* is not obvious is that the woman who wrote the novel, whose maternal ancestry was solidly Catholic, did not really think of herself that way. She saw herself as first and foremost a Southerner, and while she never failed to express her gratitude for her huge international audience, her commitment to her Southern identity was absolute, so much so that she categorically refused to get involved in making the movie for fear of upsetting or alienating the people she cared about most. As she told screenwriter Sidney Howard, one of a battery of collaborators under the supervision of Selznick (one of whom, inci-dentally, was F. Scott Fitzgerald, in the gray twilight of his career), "Southerners have been wonderful to my book and I am grateful indeed that they like it and are interested in the forthcoming picture. Not for worlds or money would I put myself in the position where if there was something they didn't like in the picture, they could say, 'Well, you worked on the script. Why did you let this that or the other get by?' I would never live it down." Mitchell was willing to accept $50,000 for the rights to her novel—the most money ever paid at the time—but that was as far as she was willing to go (although she did dispatch friends to advise Selznick and report back what was going on).

Mitchell felt no similar commitment to her childhood religion. In fact, during her freshman year of college, she decided to reject "the religious Catholic code under which I was brought up." Her most recent major biographer, Darden Asbury Pyron, explains that while her father, who had been agnostic, converted to Catholicism in 1940, and her brother, who remained faithful his entire life, talked with her about it shortly before her sudden death in a car accident in 1949, Mitchell never budged in her renunciation. "Peggy was a maverick because of religion," a friend once observed. "She used to talk about Catholics the same way some people talk about New York Jews."

To judge on the basis of the only novel she published in her lifetime, this renunciation was pretty solid. It had neither the obsessive quality one sometimes sees in those whose insistent denunciations of any former faith or cause, whether organized religion, radical politics, or a lifetime of smoking, sometimes suggests ongoing engagement, nor in the almost eerie silence that can disturb even those who did not share such aspects of a person's former life (can it be that easy, are we really that rootless, that we can simply erase parts of ourselves?). Mitchell never attempted to *hide* her religious background, and in creating arguably the most famous character in American fiction—one she used to work out many of the tensions in her own life as a woman living in the first half of the twentieth century—she made it clear that Scarlett O'Hara had both French Catholic and Irish Catholic blood. But Scarlett's religion seems like an inevitable detail accounted for by her far more decisive ethnicity, especially her Irish ancestry, than an important fact in its own right. In a novel as large and panoramic as *GWTW*, it is not surprising the subject pops up in passing a few times. But that doesn't really mean it's a Catholic book, does it?

No, it doesn't. But, you see, that's one of the most interesting things about it: that it *isn't* really a Catholic book. It tells us a lot about Margaret Mitchell, her novel, American Catholicism, and the American Dream that twines around them like vine at an antebellum plantation.

* * *

"The Klan!" [Scarlett] almost screamed it. "Ashley isn't in the Klan! Frank can't be! Oh, he promised me!"

"Of course, Mr. Kennedy is in the Klan and Ashley, too, and all the men we know," cried India. "They're men, aren't they? And white men and Southerners. You should have been proud of him instead of making him sneak out as if it were something shameful . . ."

—*Gone with the Wind*

Debutante, journalist, housewife, and novelist, Margaret Munnerlyn Mitchell was born on November 8, 1900, in Atlanta, Georgia. Her family's roots in the city run deep on both sides. Family lore has it that her paternal great–grandfather, Isaac Green Mitchell, was a circuit-riding Methodist preacher who performed the town's first wedding ceremony in the 1840s, when Atlanta was known as Marthasville, and eventually settled down there. His son, Russell Crawford Mitchell, was a hot–headed Confederate who was twice-wounded at the Battle of Antietam. He later married a Florida woman, Deborah Margaret Sweet, and became extremely successful as a cotton merchant there until fisticuffs with a man who had clout with the U.S. army of occupation led the couple to retreat back to Atlanta, where he went into the lumber business. Their eldest son, Eugene, was Margaret Mitchell's father.

Mitchell's maternal lineage, which was decisively Catholic, can be traced back to seventeenth-century Maryland. The family spread across the South from there, one branch taking root in the new cotton country of northern Georgia in the early nineteenth century. Her ethnicity was largely English—with two important exceptions. The first was her great-grandfather, Phillip Fitzgerald, who emigrated from Ireland after the abortive uprising of 1798 and whose exploits became the inspiration for Gerald O'Hara, Scarlett's boisterous father. Fitzgerald's daughter Annie, who experienced the siege of Atlanta firsthand, furnished source material for Scarlett herself, and married the other Irish immigrant in Mitchell's ancestry, John Stephens. Annie and John's daughter, Mary Isabelle (or May Belle, as she was known) was a favorite of her Fitzgerald grandparents, and was educated at a convent school in Quebec. She married Eugene Mitchell in 1892, and gave birth to two sons, only one of whom survived, before Margaret was born.

Eugene Mitchell was an attorney who lost a great deal of money in the severe economic depression that rocked the United States in 1893, and for the rest of his life he regarded maintaining his family's upper–middle class status as a struggle. According to his son Stephens, the depression took from his father "all daring and put in its place a desire to have a competence assured to him." Perhaps this is why the fathers in Mitchell's work are typically passive figures at best when it comes to dealing with their children.

The real force in Mitchell's life was clearly her mother, and an ambivalence about mothers and motherhood is also a fixture of her work. A woman of uncommon intelligence and conviction, May Belle was the president of Atlanta's most militant suffrage group. She was also a devoted wife and mother with strong traditional values. A duality between feminist self-assertion and Victorian self–abnegation was a major part of her life, as indeed it would be for her daughter.

Another major part of May Belle's life was her faith. An active churchgoer, she was also a vigorous opponent of those—and in the turn-of-the-century South there were many—who were critical of Catholicism. Catholicism has always been viewed with skepticism, if not outright hostility, in many quarters of the region, and the early decades of the twentieth century were moments of especially severe tension. Tom Watson, the incendiary agrarian populist who dominated Georgia politics of the era, was particularly anti-Catholic, and was the principal force behind a so-called convent inspection act in 1915 that led the Church to found a laymens' association to oppose it. Though it was initially limited to men, May Belle was an active force in the association, which voted to admit women three years later.

Her daughter, by contrast, seems to have had little interest in her inherited faith and the opposition it aroused. Nowhere is this more obvious than Mitchell's stance toward the Ku Klux Klan. The Klan, formed in 1866 to prevent Southern blacks from asserting their legal rights in the aftermath of the Civil War, had ebbed somewhat in the closing decades of the nineteenth century, perhaps because the passage of Jim Crow laws and more ad hoc varieties of terrorism, such as the hundreds of lynchings that took place in the 1890s, had succeeded in driving most African Americans from civil life. (One of Mitchell's most vivid childhood memories was the Atlanta race riot of 1906.) The Klan enjoyed a resurgence during the teens and twenties, spurred in part by the success of D.W. Griffith's celebrated film *Birth of a Nation* (1915), in which it was portrayed heroically, literally riding to the rescue of besieged whites. The Klan revival of the period was also notable because hatred toward Jews and Catholics became a much larger part of its focus. These newer targets effectively nationalized the organization, since such prejudices meshed well with those of Northern nativists alarmed by growing numbers of Catholics, Jews—and, especially, blacks—in their cities. Indiana, for example, was a hotbed of Klan activity in the 1920s, and the Klan was active in the defeat of Al Smith for the Democratic nomination in 1924 and in the presidential campaign of 1928, when Smith, who finally secured the nomination, lost the election to Herbert Hoover.

But the Klan was always strongest in the South. Georgia in particular was a Klan stronghold. Atlanta was known as "the imperial city of the Invisible Empire," an empire which ran a local office literally down the street where Mitchell lived for much of her life. Southern politicians routinely conferred with Klan leaders—in some cases politicians *were* Klan leaders—and while it is possible to exaggerate the power of an institution whose organization was often chaotic and whose rhetoric could be far more dramatic than its behavior, there can be little question that the Klan embodied some of the worst tendencies in American life.

None of this seemed to bother Mitchell, however. A letter to a Minnesota reader of her novel is suggestive of her attitude:

> One of the earliest purposes of the Klan was to protect women and children. Later it was used to keep the Negroes from voting eight or ten times at every election. But it was used equally against Carpetbaggers [i.e. Northerners who went South after the Civil War to exploit the region] who had the

same bad habit as far as voting was concerned. Members of the Klan knew that if unscrupulous or ignorant people were allowed to hold office in the South the lives and property would not be safe . . .

There's nothing remarkable about Mitchell's opinions here: they represented conventional wisdom as most white Southerners understood it (the fact of the matter, of course, was that most blacks were not allowed to vote once, let alone eight or ten times). Some dissident voices, notably W. E. B DuBois, whose *Black Reconstruction* (1935) is now considered a classic in the field of American history, were beginning to speak. But it would be decades before they were widely heard—though in many cases, they're still not.

How does one explain Mitchell's blithe attitude toward the Klan? Surely it has something to do with the extent of her white Southern loyalties, loyalties which, even for otherwise progressive leaders, were almost always articulated within a context of frank white supremacy (one branch of feminism, for example, has always been avowedly racist, arguing that white women were more deserving of the vote than black men). Yet this begs the question as to how Mitchell's family *could* simply assume they were like other white Southern families. Wasn't their religion a problem? The answer, apparently, is that the Catholic menace tended to be a distant abstraction rather than an immediate threat. This is a kind of pattern one sees often in American life: one or two minorities in your neighborhood isn't necessarily dangerous, especially if they've been there for a while (indeed, you can flatter yourself on your sense of tolerance). It's only when they—whoever "they" are—start moving in larger numbers and become a community in their own right that some people start to get nervous.

One intriguing hint of Mitchell's own place in her culture can be glimpsed in her treatment of the Catholic patriarch in her novel. Gerald O'Hara, it is clear, is the sole Irish Catholic man in his community, set apart by his brogue and blustery manner as much as for his religion. By some lights, he would surely be dismissed as a potato-eating arriviste. Fortunately, he has some things going for him, not the least of which is his wife Ellen, the daughter of a

Napoleonic soldier who fled the Haitian uprising of 1791 (an uprising, it's worth noting, where slaves overthrew their masters) and whose own Catholicism is impressively aristocratic. More important, his charm and desire to fit in ultimately allow him to enter WASP plantation society. As the narrator explains, "when Mrs. Wilkes, 'a great lady and with a rare gift of silence,' as Gerald characterized her, told her husband one evening, after Gerald's horse had pounded down the drive, 'He has a rough tongue, but he is a gentleman,' Gerald had definitely arrived." Years later, Gerald's funeral is officiated by Mrs. Wilkes's son Ashley, an Episcopalian, because there is no priest available in the war-torn countryside. Concerned he will confuse and anger mourners with talk of purgatory—he suspects half of those present had never heard of it and "would take it as a personal affront, if he insinuated, even in prayer, that so fine a man as Mr. O'Hara had not gone straight to heaven"—Ashley simply skips all mention of it entirely and much of the traditional Catholic funeral service in favor of more familiar Episcopal prayers and rituals. Only his wife Melanie and Scarlett's sister Careen, who is soon to join a convent, have any notion of what is really happening. To the extent that art imitates life, one suspects that if Mitchell did in fact "talk about Catholics the same way some people talk about New York Jews," it's because she didn't consider herself one, at least not the way most Southerners thought of them.

Indeed, unlike her mother, Mitchell did not receive a Catholic education. May Belle herself had left the convent rather than remain there after her sisters had graduated, and completed her own education at the Atlanta Female Institute. From a very early date, she had decided her own daughter would receive a secular education. Margaret attended a public school, a prep school, and the Washington Seminary, a finishing school founded by Baptists. The capstone of it all was to be a northern college education; Mitchell was accepted to Smith College in Northampton, Massachusetts, for the fall of 1918.

She did not stay long, however. Two cataclysmic events in her freshman year changed her life forever. The first was the death of her fiance, Lieutenant Clifford Henry, a Harvard graduate whom she met the summer before college when he trained recruits in Atlanta for the First World War and who died in France that fall.

The second and probably more decisive event was the death of her mother, a victim of the worldwide flu epidemic of 1919. After her death, Mitchell returned to Atlanta, never to resume her studies. And while there was much about her mother that continued to affect—maybe *haunt* would be a better word—Mitchell's life choices, it is clear that in many respects she took a different road to womanhood.

She did, however, show some filial devotion to her father, both in leaving school to come back home to Atlanta and giving in to pressure from him and her maternal grandmother to make a formal debut in Atlanta society so as to not ruin her marriage chances. She was approved for membership in the city's elite Debutante Club for the 1920–1921 season and was poised to become a respectable citizen.

But she never quite became respectable, at least not in the traditional way. Although Mitchell quickly made friends with other debutantes and attended a whirl of parties at country clubs, she showed clear signs of rebelling against the role in which she had been cast by smoking, drinking, and, in one much-talked-about incident, dressing in a suggestive Apache costume for a ball. In response, she was pointedly overlooked by the Junior League. Despite her iconoclasm, Mitchell was deeply hurt by the slight, and exacted revenge years later by declining to attend the Junior League's ball in her honor during the film premiere of *GWTW*.

The conflicting tensions in Mitchell's life coalesced in her relationship with another pivotal figure in her life: Berrien, or "Red" Upshaw. Upshaw came from a respectable Georgia family, but there was an air of scandal about him. He twice "voluntarily resigned" from the U.S. Naval Academy in Annapolis, and after his parents cut him off financially, he was apparently able to support himself at the University of Georgia by bootlegging. Despite vigorous opposition from family and friends, Mitchell married Upshaw in 1922.

Upshaw's best man was his roommate John Marsh, a quiet, retiring World War I veteran who stood in sharp contrast to his rakish friend. Marsh had also made a bid for Mitchell's affections, but after her engagement to Upshaw, he accepted a role as trusted friend for both bride and groom. When the marriage got off to a rocky

start on the honeymoon and remained tense thereafter, Marsh medi-
ated for the couple. After fights over money, Upshaw's drinking, and
his lack of a steady job, the two agreed to a divorce, and Upshaw
abruptly left Mitchell. Occasionally he returned, most notably a few
months later, when he assaulted her so brutally that she required
weeks to recover. Upshaw died after leaping from the fifth-story
window of a Texas hotel in 1949, months before Mitchell's own
death.

Lacking financial support from Upshaw, and reluctant to
depend on her father, Mitchell landed a job at the *Atlanta Journal* as
a feature writer for the paper's Sunday magazine in 1922. Meanwhile, she and Marsh became increasingly close. In 1925 she married
him, leaving her father's home for an apartment in downtown
Atlanta. Injuries and ailments of the kind that were to plague her
and Marsh for the rest of their lives led her to quit the paper, and
Marsh's job as a publicist for the Georgia Power Company provided
financial stability. Long interested in fiction writing, Mitchell began
working on the book that became *GWTW*.

Mitchell kept her ambitions under wraps for a long time. By
1929 she had essentially written a draft of the novel and, although
her family and friends were aware she was doing *something* at home,
no one but Marsh was quite aware of the scope of her ambitions
(she kept her typewriter covered with a bath towel and called writing "therapy for my [injured] leg"). In 1935 a friend in publishing
told New York editor Harold Latham, who was going south to scout
talent, about Mitchell's work; he sought her out but was persistently
refused a look at the manuscript. It was only when an acquaintance
reputedly expressed surprise that Michell was "the type to write a
novel" and suggested she "lacked the seriousness necessary to be a
novelist" that an indignant Mitchell chased down Latham just as he
was about to catch a train back to New York. The rest, of course, is
history.

As even this brief survey suggests, Margaret Mitchell's life was
rife with conflicts—over family obligations to both her parents; over
men who were idealized and/or unavailable on the one hand, passive and/or needy on the other; over personal assertiveness and a
desire to belong—that eventually found their way into her fiction,

particularly in the figure of Scarlett O'Hara. These tensions have been examined in detail by a number of writers, myself among them. Yet relatively little has been written about one tension Mitchell herself said relatively little about: Catholicism. Though *GWTW* is obviously about many other things, it's finally about that too, and bears some examination for what it reveals about the distinctive ways in which people choose to reject their religion in their quest for the American Dream.

* * *

When Scarlett was a child, she had confused her mother with the Virgin Mary, and now that she was older she saw no reason for changing her opinion.

—Gone with the Wind

Scarlett's dream is clear enough: She wants Ashley Wilkes. And to get him, she's willing to do virtually anything, even midwife the child of her saintly rival, Melanie Wilkes. But when *GWTW* opens, Ashley is not quite the dominant figure in Scarlett's life. Her mother, Ellen, is.

In fact, Scarlett adores her mother—to the point of sacrilege. We first see them together in the fourth chapter of the novel, when Ellen has returned from tending to the illegitimate child of Emmie Slattery and the O'Hara family's plantation overseer, Jonas Wilkerson. "Is the brat baptized?" Gerald asks. "Yes, and dead, poor thing," Ellen replies. "I feared Emmie would die too, but I think she will live." (Ironically, it is because Emmie lives that Ellen dies; she contracts typhoid while tending to Emmie later in the story.) Gerald laments that the child is fatherless—a misperception that Ellen will soon correct by ordering him to fire Wilkerson—but for the moment she directs the gathered family to begin evening prayers. Only one person has the power to distract her as she reaches for her rosary beads: Mammy, who demands that she eat. Thus the family has dinner before Ellen begins the Litany of the Virgin. Gerald is clearly unenthusiastic about this ritual, but Scarlett is not:

"The kneeling figures, the soft glow of the lamp, the dim shadows where the negroes swayed, even the familiar objects that had been so hateful to her sight an hour ago, in an instant took on the color of her own emotions, and the room seemed once more a lovely place. She would never forget this moment or this scene!" At the center of it all was Ellen. "Sacrilegious though it might be, Scarlett always saw, through her closed eyes, the upturned face of Ellen and not the Blessed Virgin, as the ancient phrases were repeated."

The problem for Scarlett is that Ellen is a tough act to follow. (Significantly, the one person who does measure up, Melanie Wilkes, is described by Rhett at the end of the book very similarly to the way Ellen is at the beginning: "a great lady.")[7] Ellen's eldest daughter, however, is another story. "Scarlett wanted very much to be like her mother," the narrator explains at the end of the third chapter with just a hint of puckishness. "The only difficulty was that by being just and truthful and tender and unselfish, one missed most of the joys of life, and certainly many beaux. And life was too short to miss such pleasant things. Some day when she was married to Ashley and old, some day when she had time for it, she intended to be like Ellen. But until then . . ." There the chapter ends, suspended in a sinful present.

Scarlett is aware that she is not like her mother, and it creates a powerful sense of dissonance. Still, initially at least, she can overcome it. "Ellen would be shocked and grieved to know that a daughter of hers wanted a man who was engaged to another girl," Scarlett thinks. "But, in the depths of the first tragedy she had ever known, she wanted the very comfort of her mother's presence. She always felt secure when Ellen was by her, for there was nothing so bad that Ellen could not better it, simply by being there."

By this point in the story, the reader knows something Scarlett never does: that her mother had *herself* once been a headstrong girl who also knew the anguish of forbidden love. Young Ellen Robillard had been deeply involved with her cousin Phillippe, "a wild buck" that her family had been after her "morning and night" to give up. When Phillippe gets killed in a barroom brawl in New Orleans, which Ellen learns about from a letter by a priest, she renounces her once youthful passions to marry Gerald O'Hara. O'Hara can barely believe his luck. No doubt Scarlett would be fascinated to learn this family secret (Mammy, who knows it, remains resolutely mum), but it probably would not have done her any good: having renounced her own happiness, Ellen would surely have insisted Scarlett do the same. And Scarlett, it is abundantly clear even as she's praying with her mother and the rest of the family, has no intention of doing so. In fact, she's laying the groundwork for her campaign to capture Ashley even as Ellen recites the Litany of the Virgin.

Over the course of the novel, circumstances push Scarlett away from Ellen, literally as well as figuratively. Widowed after her brief marriage to Melanie's brother Charles, Scarlett is sent to visit relatives early on in the Civil War, making her way from boring Charleston and Savannah to bustling Atlanta. Here she is truly in her element. We see her, for example, at the Confederate ball, discarding conventions of mourning to dance with Rhett Butler and donating her unwanted wedding band to an army auction (actions for which Melanie provides cover by donating her own, much more cherished, wedding band). One of the more interesting aspects of this moment of Confederate high tide, a moment that Scarlett enjoys as much as anyone, is that she nevertheless reveals a sense of skepticism about the war that she will retain throughout the book. And that skepticism, if somewhat immature, is also informed by a religious perspective:

> . . . Even the banked flowers below the pictures of Mr. [Jefferson] Davis and Mr. [Alexander] Stephens displeased her.
>
> "It looks like an altar," she sniffed. "And they way they all carry on about those two, they might as well be the Father and the Son!" Then smitten with sudden fright at her irreverence, she began hastily to cross herself by way of apology but caught herself in time.
>
> "Well it's true," she argued with her conscience. "Everybody carries on like they were holy and they aren't anything but men, and mighty unattractive looking ones at that."

This is a good snapshot of Scarlett's religious profile, sugges-tive of the way in which she retains a religious frame of reference and an instinctive sense of guilt that accompanies her irrepressible pragmatism.

Scarlett's sense of guilt becomes steadily more pressing, and peaks when she receives a letter from her mother reproaching her for her behavior at the ball. "I am heartbroken to think you could so soon forget your rearing," Ellen writes. "I hope and pray it was only youth and recklessness that prompted such forward conduct." Sig-nificantly, Scarlett does not even finish reading the letter: she'd simply rather not know. She does read enough to learn that Ellen has dis-patched Gerald to confront Rhett, a prospect that fills her with horror: "She wished she were dead, this very minute, then everyone would be sorry they were so hateful." Presumably, Scarlett is referring to herself here, but the grammar of the sentence is such that she could at least theoretically be referring to Ellen as well (for Ellen's death would quiet all the wagging tongues that surround Scarlett).[8] Scarlett could never admit wanting her mother dead—her Catholic conscience would be genuinely mortified at the thought—but the locution is nevertheless suggestive of the way oppressive standards can give rise to unconscious wishes.

As it turns out, Scarlett need not have worried: Rhett so thor-oughly charms her father with cards and alcohol that Scarlett can blackmail Gerald (who is hung over and $500 poorer) to reassure Ellen that all the talk about Rhett and their daughter was nothing more than vicious rumor. But Scarlett has by this point thoroughly internalized her mother's judgment—not in a way that will lead her to change her behavior, mind you, only in a way that makes her feel bad about it. The clever techniques she uses to manipulate people, her mother included, cannot altogether quiet the two dominant emo-tions she associates with her mother and the religious heritage Ellen so vividly embodies. The first of these is guilt.

The other? Anxiety. We see this most clearly when Scarlett learns Ellen is ill and she resorts to a strategy common among even other-wise atheistic people: hard bargaining. With Atlanta about to fall to Union forces, and Melanie about to give birth to her son, a dis-traught Scarlett reflects with bitter amazement on her situation:

> Dear God! Suppose she [Melanie] should die? Melanie dead. Melanie dead. And Ashley—No, I mustn't think about that, it isn't nice. But Ashley—No, I mustn't think about that because he's probably dead, anyway. But he made me promise I'd take care of her. But—if I didn't take care of her and she died and Ashley is still alive—No, I mustn't think about that. It's sinful. And I promised God I'd be good if He would just not let mother die.

What is most interesting about Scarlett's repeated injunction that she "mustn't think about that" is how instrumental her thinking is. Sure, such thoughts are sinful, but in the end the real reason not to think them is that they may upset her unwritten contracts with Ashley and God. And as long as they don't explicitly violate the terms, she'll keep up her end.

But God, who was never an explicit signatory to the deal, does not honor it: Ellen dies. For Scarlett, this is one of a series of blows that includes the destruction wrought by General Sherman's hated army, the senility of her father, and the crushing burden of rebuilding Tara. The cumulative impact of these experiences permanently changes her—she develops a leaner, meaner psyche and sheds excess baggage. "Nothing her mother had taught her was of any value whatsoever now and Scarlett's heart was sore and puzzled," she thinks to herself.

Among the things now gone with the wind are the piety and beauty of her mother's Catholicism. Henceforth, Scarlett will be a skeptic. "Occasionally, Scarlett wondered bitterly why Melanie could not have died in childbirth in Atlanta," she reflects later. "That would have made things perfect. Then she could have married Ashley after a decent interval and made Beau a good stepmother too. When such thoughts came she did not pray hastily to God, telling him she did not mean it. God did not frighten her anymore." Nor is she inclined to strike any more deals, and reacts with irritation to her sister Careen's piety. "If God had seen fit to punish them so, then God could do very well without prayers," she thinks. As the narrator explains, "Religion had always been a bargaining process with Scarlett. She promised God good behavior in exchange for favors.

God had broken the bargain time and again, to her way of thinking, and she felt that she owed him nothing at all now."

Nowhere is Scarlett's distant relationship with God more apparent than in her relationship with her children, which is also quite distant. In fact, Rhett seems to care more about Scarlett's children by her other husbands that Scarlett herself does. "The congregation of the Episcopal Church almost fell out of their pews when he tiptoed in, late for services, with Wade's [her son by her first husband] hand in his," we're told. "The congregation was as much stunned by Wade's appearance as by Rhett's, for the little boy was supposed to be Catholic. At least, Scarlett was one. Or she was supposed to be one. But she had not put foot in the church in years, for religion had gone from her as many of Ellen's other teaching's had gone."

Far more shocking is Scarlett's reaction to learning she is pregnant with a child by Rhett: she indicates she's considering an abortion. Only Rhett's anguished description of the medical dangers lead her to change her mind. When, with their marriage deeply estranged, she later finds herself pregnant again, an angry Scarlett tells Rhett, "Oh, God, I wish it was anybody's baby but yours!" Rhett replies with sarcasm that may also accurately reflect her true feelings: "'Cheer up,' he said, turning from her and starting up the stairs, 'maybe you'll have a miscarriage.'" One senses the hand of an angry God as an infuriated Scarlett lunges for Rhett, misses, and falls down those stairs, precipitating that very miscarriage.

Still, old habits die hard, and as the story proceeds it's clear that Scarlett's angst–ridden Catholic conscience has not altogether vanished. In a rare moment of remorse, she reflects on her poor behavior with her second husband, Frank Kennedy. "God would punish her for not being nicer to him—punish her for all her bullyings and proddings and storms of temper and cutting remarks." There's nothing conditional about this: it *will* happen, and Scarlett *is* terrified. Rhett, the voice of reason, tries to talk her out of it by pointing out that she believed God would understand other decisions she'd made; why not marrying Frank? "Rhett, how can you talk about God when you know you don't believe there is one?" she asks him impatiently at one point. "But you believe in a God of Wrath and that's what's important at present," he replies. "I'm surprised at you,

Scarlett, for sprouting a conscience this late in life. Opportunists like you shouldn't have them." In thinking that Scarlett's conscience is a new thing, Rhett here betrays a little of the clouded vision that tragically dooms his own marriage to Scarlett (as does his failure to trust, as Melanie does, that Scarlett really loves him). But he's surely correct that Scarlett's faith, as currently constituted, doesn't do much good for anyone.

Scarlett makes one last bid to come to terms with that God of Wrath when a group of observers witness a genuinely chaste embrace between her and Ashley and are scandalized by what they think they see. By this point, though, Scarlett doesn't really care about what anybody thinks—except Melanie. "She was driven by a conscience which, though long suppressed, could still rise up, an active Catholic conscience," the narrator reports as she arrives for a surprise birthday party for Ashley at the Wilkes's house.

> "Confess your sins and do penance for them in sorrow and contrition," Ellen had told her a hundred times, and in this crisis, Ellen's religious training came back and gripped her. She would confess—yes, everything, every look and word, those few caresses—and then God would ease her pain and give her peace. And, for her penance, there would be the dreadful sight of Melanie's face changing from fond love and trust to incredulous horror and repulsion. Oh, that was too hard a penance, she thought in anguish, to have to live out her life remembering Melanie's face, knowing that Melanie knew all the pettiness, the meanness, the two-faced disloyalty and the hypocrisy that were in her."

Scarlett simply can't bring herself to confess, which is probably just as well: Melanie may in fact already know the truth and have made a considered choice to ignore it. (This is one of those ambiguities that makes *GWTW* such a fascinating story.) In any event, the only reason Scarlett has these thoughts in the first place is because Rhett made her go to the party—for reasons that may reflect a correct reading of Melanie's desires in the matter—and his desire to see Scarlett squirm. Indeed, you might say Rhett understands his wife's lingering Catholicism better than she does. "I'm sure I can't see why she [Melanie] loves you but she does," he tells Scarlett coldly. "Let that be one of your crosses." Later, he alludes to the Gospel of Matthew: "'Lusting in your heart.' That's a good phrase, isn't it? There are a number of good phrases in that Book, aren't there?" Typically, a clueless Scarlett has no idea what he's talking about.

Actually, her confused, painful thoughts about Melanie bring us to the heart of the matter: Scarlett can never recapture a sense of religion as something *other* than suffering, guilt, and anxiety for herself and others. Her faith, like so many other aspects of her life, is emotionally stunted. And it is this more than anything that may finally be the heaviest cross that she bears.

Scarlett is not entirely without spiritual resources, however. "Remember, she doesn't know anything," she tells Ashley as Melanie is dying from her failed quest to have a second child. "She never even suspected—God was that good to us." Her grief over Melanie's death is as honest an emotion as Scarlett experiences in the entire book, and is notably absent of the anger and calculation that characterized so much of her relationship with God. But it's that sense of absence—of *any* real relationship—that's finally most evident. It's not so much that Scarlett has wholly rejected any kind of religious life; it's simply been suspended.

In that regard, the religious tenor of *GWTW* is consonant with the spirit of the story as a whole: a lack of resolution goes to the heart of what it's all about. Once again, it is Rhett who succinctly summarizes Scarlett's life, this time her American Dream: "Ever since I've known you, you've wanted two things. Ashley and to be rich enough to tell the world to go to hell. Well, you are rich enough and you've spoken sharply to the world and you've got Ashley, if you want him. But all that doesn't seem to be enough now." Scarlett's response is revealing: "She was frightened but not at the thought of hell fire." What she now fears is losing Rhett. For Scarlett, the American Dream recedes infinitely into the distance, its attainment never quite as satisfying as the quest—or the next landmark on the horizon.

It is this as much as anything that makes Scarlett O'Hara a quintessential American figure. Earthly goals seem much more appealing and attainable than heavenly ones, but as often as not finally prove even more elusive whether or not they are achieved. Catholics have proven as susceptible to such mirages as anyone. "Happy? I don't know," a meditative Frank Sinatra, himself a lapsed Catholic for most his life, once responded to a query about the days before he became a gigantic star. "I wasn't *un*happy, let's put it that way. I never had it so good. Sometimes I wonder whether anybody had it like I had it, before or since. It's was the damnedest thing, wasn't it? But I was too busy ever to know whether I was happy or even to ask myself." He also seemed too busy ruining his once gorgeous voice with smoking and drinking, abusing many of those who loved him most, and spending far too much time with the wrong kind of people to reconsider the value of his attained American Dream and the price he had paid for it. I say this less to join the chorus of people who have justly or unjustly criticized Sinatra's lifestyle—we can only hope he finally made his peace with God before his death in 1998—than to suggest that as exceptional a figure as he was in many ways, Sinatra, like Scarlett O'Hara, nevertheless remains emblematic of a certain kind of Catholic denial that has been widely prevalent in American culture for a long time.

Meanwhile, Scarlett O'Hara, like all fictional characters, lives in the eternal present. Will she get Rhett back? Will she finally be able to integrate the spirits of the angelically otherworldly Ellen and Melanie with her own spirited worldliness? In other words: Will Scarlett finally grow up? Part of what makes the story so compelling is that it ends without our ever really knowing. Perhaps Margaret Mitchell realized that, like the Dream itself, her story would be more durable if it was somehow not quite finished.

In any event, we certainly have hope. Scarlett is only twenty-eight when the book ends. People do not usually change significantly during their lifetime, but Christianity as a whole is premised on the idea that it is always *possible*. We have hope for Scarlett; we have hope for ourselves. Our denials are often emphatic. But they are rarely complete.

BORDERLINE CATHOLIC

Madonna strikes a pose for her 1985 film *Desperately Seeking Susan*. Note the prominently situated crucifix she wears, a staple of her wardrobe at the time. Frequently glib, if not sacrilegious, about her Catholic heritage, a strong vein of spiritual engagement animates Madonna's best work, notably her 1989 song, album, and video *Like a Prayer*. *(Photo by Herb Ritts courtesy of The Kobal Collection, New York)*

Chapter Five

LIKE A HERETIC:
THE CASE OF MADONNA

I won't be happy until I'm as famous as God.

—Madonna Louise Ciccone

It's difficult to take Madonna—the American Madonna, that is, the one dubbed "our lady of constant makeovers" by *USA Today*—seriously. Not that an extraordinary variety of people haven't tried. In fact, that's part of the problem: so many have, with such embarrassing results. On one end of the spectrum are conservatives who decry her work and behavior with stridence, mindlessness, or both. ("The freeing of the priest from the bondage of being locked up in the building is good. Christianity should not be locked up in the building," wrote Donald Wildmon, director of the American Family Association, in a painfully literal-minded, and otherwise denunciatory, analysis of one of her videos). At the other are self-styled academic radicals who turned Madonna into a cottage industry in the 1990s with articles whose mere titles—"Embodying Subaltern Memory: Kinesthesia and the Problematics of Gender and Race," or "Power to the Pussy: We Don't Want to Be Wannabe Dicks in Drag"—are incomprehensible, laughable, or both. Writer/director Quentin Tarantino, in a semi-earnest satire of these impulses, opens his 1992 film *Reservoir Dogs* with a group of criminals in a diner arguing over the implications of Madonna's famous 1984 song "Like a Virgin."

I'm not saying that Madonna, or, for that matter, any other pop culture icon, isn't worthy of sustained commentary (given my own track record, I'd be a hypocrite if I did). Nor am I saying that there hasn't been some intelligent analysis from many quarters, ranging from *The Nation* on the left to *The National Review* on the right. The difficulty in trying to add much is relatively great, not only because so much, good and bad, has already been said, but also because it's easy to look silly talking rationally about essentially irrational matters like sex and to trivialize important matters like spirituality in the process of doing so.

In terms of the American Dream, Madonna is neither the first nor the last person to rise from modest circumstances to the summit of fame and fortune in a success–obsessed society like the United States. Nor were her means, which principally involved using her body, unique. But few figures in American life have managed to exert as much control over their destinies as she has, and the fact that she has done so as a woman is all the more remarkable (even at this late date, one suspects that much of the antipathy that Madonna has generated would not be nearly as pronounced if she were a man, for whom words like "ambition" still do not have quite the same negative overtones that they do for women). Indeed, it is people like her—Oprah Winfrey is another—who seem to demonstrate the ongoing vitality and legitimacy of the American Dream by proving that it remains relevant, desirable, and, above all, achievable for people who have been marginalized for much of our history.

That Madonna has done this is indisputable. That she has done so as a Roman Catholic—well, that *is* disputable. No one denies that she was baptized into the Church and that her religion was a significant part of her upbringing. Indeed, admirers and critics alike agree that it was the very intensity of that upbringing that led her to rebel against it, and that much of her appeal stems from the degree to which she has flouted traditional notions of piety. While Madonna has not been formally excommunicated from the Church, the Vatican has condemned her work—her reaction to this news is dramatized in the 1991 documentary *Truth or Dare*—and many feel that her behavior has been so patently sacrilegious that it would be a travesty to regard Madonna as anything other than an apostate.

The fact that Madonna herself has always considered herself Catholic, and has been abundantly quoted to that effect, is somewhat beside the point (Madonna has said many things over the course of her surprisingly long career, and not even she would have us believe all of them.) But a close look at her work does suggest a surprising degree of genuine religious engagement, nowhere more obviously in *Like a Prayer*—a song, video, and album of the same name she released in 1989. As far as fidelity to traditional church practice goes, she's no role model. In fact the outcry surrounding the video in particular was so pronounced that Pepsi, which sponsored a commercial featuring the song, decided not to broadcast it for fear of offending religious leaders and laity. But in her longings and habits, Madonna is an exceptionally revealing example of a certain *kind* of American Catholic, and suggestive of the ways in which a Catholic identity shapes even those most insistent on rejecting its core tenets. It may not be true that once you're a Catholic you're always a Catholic. But if nothing else, Madonna shows that it isn't easy to be a bona fide apostate.

✽   ✽   ✽

I sometimes think I was born to live up to my name. How could I be anything else but what I am, having been named Madonna? I would either have ended up a nun or this.

She always liked nuns. She spoke of them repeatedly throughout her career. "Growing up I thought nuns were very beautiful," she told a reporter during an interview for *Time* magazine in 1985. "For several years I wanted to be a nun, and I got very close to them in grade school and junior high. I saw them as really pure, disciplined, sort of above–average people. They never wore any makeup and they had these really serene faces. Nuns are sexy."

Reading these words on a printed page (as opposed to having the benefit of her tone and facial expression), it's not altogether clear just how to take "nuns are sexy." Is this: a) calculated outrage by a shameless publicity hound; b) an unselfconscious, if somewhat immature, remark from someone who, unlike many Catholics, does not feel compelled to strictly segregate sacred and sexual experience; c) a matter-of-fact statement of the truth, that in the purity of their devotion to Christ, a devotion often notable for its wholeness and intensity, nuns sometimes do exhibit a mysterious sexual magnetism?

My guess is "a." But in a larger sense it doesn't matter: whatever the correct answer—and you can posit your own "d"—it seems clear that Madonna's commentary is rooted in more–than–casual firsthand experience. Noting that nuns were "above average" people, lacked makeup, and had serene faces does not constitute the most scintillating analysis one can imagine, but such statements are clearly rooted in close personal observation that she related years later as part of a discussion of childhood idols that included Carole Lombard and Marilyn Monroe. The factual record and subjective recollection are in accord: here is a child of the Church.

Madonna Louise Veronica Ciccone (pronounced in Florentine Italian: "Chiconey") was born in Bay City, Michigan, on August 16, 1958, the oldest daughter and third of six children. Yes, "Madonna" is really her Christian name, and given the future trajectory of her career, it's hard to imagine her coming up with a more provocative one. ("It wasn't until I came to New York that I became aware it was such an unusual name. People just assumed it was a stage name," she has said.) She got it from her mother, Madonna Fortin, a French Canadian. Though the name "Jesus," for example, is not uncommon in Latin Catholic circles, "Madonna" is, and it's even more unusual for a mother to name her daughter after herself the way men often name their sons.[9] But if Madonna Fortin's role in shaping her daughter's fate is obvious, it is also elusive: she died of cancer in December 1963, when Madonna was five years old. Not surprisingly, mothers, mothering, and motherhood haunt the younger Madonna's life and work.

In a very different way, so do fathers, fathering, and fatherhood. Silvio Ciccone was the youngest of six boys, a child of Italian immigrants who settled outside Pittsburgh. His father worked in steel mills, but the upwardly mobile Silvio served in the Air Force, received an engineering degree, and moved to Michigan, where he prospered in the automotive industry. It was there that he met Madonna's mother; after her death he remarried and had two more children. While Madonna describes herself as her father's favorite, being the oldest girl in a highly traditional household was apparently burdensome as well. "I feel like my childhood was spent taking care of babies and changing diapers and baby-sitting," she recalled years later. "I think that's when I really thought about how I wanted to do something else and get away from all that. I really saw myself as the quintessential Cinderella."

For better and worse, her father also set the tone of her spiritual life. A number of observers of Madonna's work have argued that the expressiveness, even the profanity, of her work is rooted in the earthy style of working-class Italian Catholicism. There's a lot of truth to this. But her descriptions of her childhood religious practice seem far closer to a lace-curtain Irish, even Puritan, experience. "We used to get up every morning and go to church for an hour before school," Madonna, who attended parochial schools throughout her childhood, told *Interview* magazine in 1989. "It just seemed like such torture—school was punishment enough." Moreover, Silvio Ciccone was very much a proponent of the Protestant work ethic. "I don't know if this was my father or Catholicism, but I was also raised to believe that idle time wasn't good. You always had to be doing something productive, either your schoolwork or prayer or housework, never sitting around and having too much leisure time. You always had to be challenging your mind and body, and that has definitely shaped my adult life." Madonna's sculpted physique is an ironic affirmation of the degree to which she internalized this cult of discipline, if not quite in the way her father imagined.

Actually, the ways in which she strayed from her heritage are far more obvious than the ways she affirmed it. The rebellions came early. "I remember I wanted to chase after boys on the playground, and the nuns told me I couldn't: that good Catholic girls didn't chase boys," she explained. "I didn't understand what was so bad about it, so I would do it anyway. And I would get punished for it." The fact that this conflict was taking place at a parochial school no doubt intensified her growing antipathy for Catholicism, but such struggles were also being fought at home and at Mass, all of which were intertwined. " I also remember being really annoyed that I couldn't wear pants to school or church. I kept saying to my father, 'But why can't I love God the same way if I have pants on?' [laughs] You know?

And my father would always have these stock responses, like 'Because I said so.'"

These seemingly trivial arguments led to more fundamentally doctrinal ones. As she continued in the revealing *Interview* session: "I got into this whole thing with my father about: Why do I have to go to church to pray? Why can't I take the basic principles of this religion—principles like being good and doing unto others as you would have them do unto you—and *live* them? Why do I have to go to confession to confess my sins? Why can't I just tell God directly?" One answer, of course, is that there *was* no reason she had to do things like pray in church or go to confession, except that if she didn't she would no longer be a practicing Catholic. The very logic of such questions, which must have been repeated countless of times by children all over the country for decades, are a vivid illustration of the way in which the freedom–loving, pragmatic tenor of American life gives it an instinctively Protestant cast even for cradle Catholics.

And for Madonna, as with countless other children, these questions, unsatisfactorily answered, led to action: she left—home, school, and the Church.

A dancer since she was fourteen, she was smart and talented enough to be admitted to the University of Michigan, but stayed for only one year. The oft–told story of her next move—a 1978 flight to New York and a cab ride to Times Square with thirty-seven dollars in her purse—has an archetypal quality. Relying on the kindness, if that's what it was, of a stranger who put her up in his apartment for two weeks, she got a job at Dunkin' Donuts and found a cheap apartment in the then–dangerous East Village. ("I was afraid, I didn't know if I had done the right thing. I missed my family, and then I'd say, well, at least I don't have to go to church every Sunday," she later remembered.) When she heard that choreographer Pearl Lang, cofounder of the fabled Alvin Ailey dance troupe, was holding a workshop in North Carolina, Madonna scrounged up the bus fare and went. Once there, she walked up to a table and said she was auditioning solely for the opportunity to work with Lang and feigned surprise to learn she was actually speaking to the famed choreographer. At the end of the first week of classes, Madonna boldly asked if she could join the company back in New York. She did—as part of the third-string troupe.

Perhaps predictably, Madonna was restless with such lowly status. She switched from the classes she was taking with Ailey to Lang's own company, but found her approach too "painful, dark, and guilt ridden. Very Catholic." Before long, she was looking for other outlets for her volcanic ambition—ambition that perhaps was greater than her talent. Sensing that her future might not lie solely in dance, Madonna became interested in pop music. A boyfriend, Dan Gilroy, introduced her to two French producers behind the international pop star Patrick Hernandez. Impressed by her potential, they brought Madonna to Paris in May 1979, where she worked as a backup singer and dancer. But when that didn't bring the hoped-for rewards, she returned to New York three months later and became a drummer in the Breakfast Club, Gilroy's band. After an acting stint in *A Certain Sacrifice*, a low-budget erotic thriller, in 1980, Madonna teamed up with an old Ann Arbor beau, Stephen Bray, to write some songs (in her collaborations with Bray and other songwriters, Madonna was principally the lyricist). She attracted the attention of an influential disk jockey, Mark Kamins, who played her demo tape at Danceteria, a hot New York nightclub. Kamins, who was also Madonna's lover, secured her a contract with Warner Brothers, and produced her first record, "Everybody," which made a splash in club circles in 1982. But it was not until she began working with yet another beau, the well-known pop producer John "Jellybean" Benitez, that she was poised to break into the musical mainstream. Her first album, *Madonna*, was released in July 1983.

It was not an auspicious debut. The first single from the album, "Holiday," managed to eke its way into the *Billboard* top twenty by the end of the year, but neither critics nor audiences seemed much impressed. Though professionally produced and rich with melodic hooks, qualities for which Benitez and other collaborators should get much of the credit, Madonna's lyrics were utterly conventional, even trite ("you shine on me wherever you are," went one typical line from the song "Lucky Star"). Nor has she ever been much of a singer. Writing years later in another context, British sociologist Simon Frith—arguably the best pop music critic on either

side of the Atlantic—wrote with notable clarity about her limitations as a singer: "Madonna's voice is a thin instrument. There's not
much body in it; her vocal chords don't, in themselves, make enough
noise to defy a rhythm track. She gets her effects not by switching
gear but by switching register, and, whether she's singing from mouth
or throat or chest, when she pushes her voice it becomes shrill and
slightly petulant." Of course, popular music has rarely been a
terrain of musicological excellence—it is precisely the ragged thin-
ness of Bob Dylan's voice, for instance, that gives it authenticity—but
even by this standard, Madonna comes up short. I myself remember
thinking that her near-exact musical contemporary, Cyndi Lauper,
whose delightfully nasal but undeniably powerful Brooklynese in
songs like "Girls Just Want to Have Fun" dominated the airwaves in
mid-eighties, would have a far longer, more durable career. Yet by
decade's end it was clear that Lauper had become a historical curio,
and Madonna—whose commercial demise was regularly predicted
by those who had seen countless musical fads come and go—had
become a cultural force to be reckoned with.

Why did this happen? There are a number of reasons. One is
that Madonna had the good fortune to arrive at the onset of the
MTV era. Music Television, which debuted in 1981, profoundly
transformed the music industry in the 1980s, restructuring the commercial and cultural standards of success. The most obvious
dimension of this realignment was the new visual orientation of popular music. To be sure, Frank Sinatra, Elvis Presley, or the Beatles
were hardly unattractive, but now more than ever, how one *looked*
became at least as important as how one *sounded*. This was not
simply a matter of sex appeal, although that was hardly incidental; a
sense of ease before the camera, acting ability, and skills such as
dancing—which gained more prominence than it had in twenty
years—became paramount. All of these factors worked to Madonna's
benefit.

There were also more subtle ramifications to the MTV explo-
sion. One was a new emphasis on hits. Ever since the Beatles' heyday,
pop music was virtually synonymous with rock and roll, and rock
and roll was a musical genre rooted in *albums*. The disco craze of
the seventies to some degree challenged that order, but did not

overthrow it. In MTV's wake, however, individual *songs* gained new primacy, and new musical genres, like hip–hop, offered compelling alternatives to rock. Moreover, while the traditional rock music of the seventies and eighties emphasized continuity and sincerity (e.g., Bruce Springsteen), the visual emphasis of MTV placed a premium on visual novelty; its fascination with surface appearances, rapid transitions, and endless recombinations of previously established cultural references made music video the quintessential example of what scholars mean when they refer to postmodernism. Here too were cultural criteria that played to Madonna's strengths.

Finally, ideological factors worked in Madonna's favor. Her ascendance coincided with the heart of the Reagan presidency, a period of notable cultural and political conservatism. In one sense, of course, Madonna's ambition, assertiveness, and sexuality were anything but conservative. For her, as for most other Americans of her generation, the transformations of the 1960s marked a watershed in social mores, and there was no going back. Indeed, notwithstanding the complaints on the part of some figures in the womens' movement, there is little question that Madonna was a feminist, if you define the term as a belief in the efficacy of women asserting their power in society. But unlike earlier generations of feminists who sought equality *with* men, Madonna staked her power in terms of difference *from* men, viewing sex not as a source of subordination but rather as the means to assert and justify womens' wishes and actions. To illustrate this point, consider that one never sees Madonna as interacting with others in a workplace, participating in some kind of civic activity such as voting, or sharing childcare duties, images which would typify the values of equality feminism. When, in her 1989 video for "Express Yourself," she dons a business suit, she boldly subverts its effect with fashionable slits that emphasize her cleavage. Her ultimate power, even when it is emotional and intellectual power, is rooted in womanhood. This emphasis on difference feminism is the thread that ties together the various public personas—waif, bombshell, dominatrix, even mother—that Madonna has embraced over the course of her career.

These various cultural strands—the pop music situation of the early eighties, postmodernism, and feminism—crystallized in 1984 with the release of her videos for "Borderline" and "Lucky Star," two songs that entered the *Billboard* top ten in the spring and fall respectively. The latter, an arrestingly simple production of dancers against a completely white background, showcased Madonna's sexual allure, while the former, a story video about a romance between Madonna's character and a Latino man, established a recurrent pattern of drawing on Latin accents in her work (as in her 1986 hit single and video "La Isla Bonita"). After a wobbly start, her career finally began to take hold.

But it was the release of her album *Like a Virgin*—and, in particular, two notorious videos, "Like a Virgin" and "Material Girl," which dominated the airwaves during 1984 and 1985—that completed Madonna's transition from an up-and-coming pop star to full-blown cultural phenomenon. Newspaper columnists argued about her. Young girls who dressed like her—so-called Madonna wannabees—stalked local malls. And with her starring role in *Desperately Seeking Susan* and marriage to the tempestuous actor Sean Penn in 1985, Madonna became even more inescapable. The release of her 1986 album *True Blue*, which spawned a series of hit songs and videos, consolidated her place as the premier pop singer of her time—and, perhaps, the most famous woman in the world.

If there was one thing everyone could agree on amid all the debate and hype, it was that Madonna was simply outrageous, a woman dedicated to subverting any and all versions of conventional wisdom. In retrospect, though, it's clear that the pull of the past, of tradition, was more decisive than many of us realized. No one—no one that wants to become famous as an entertainer, anyway—can wholly reject the standards and expectations of her audience. When Madonna sang "feels so good inside" during a performance of "Like a Virgin" while wearing a wedding dress, as she did at the 1985 MTV Awards, the electric charge was not simply due to her highly suggestive writhing—lots of performers do that, whether in strip clubs or on MTV. It was also in the way the performance emphasized, even revitalized, some of our most common cultural conventions, from the lyrics of pop songs (where "feels so good inside" is a virtual cliché) to marital rituals (where it's easy to forget that sex is a sacramental act).

This strategy of couching cultural transgression against a back-drop of tradition, even morality, is a fixture of Madonna's work. The *song* for "Material Girl" insouciantly celebrates frank sexual exploitation ("Only boys who spend their pennies make my rainy day"), while the *video* shows that it is the nice poor boy (or at least the film director who *acts* like a nice poor boy) who gets the girl. In both the song *and* video for "Papa Don't Preach," a depiction of out-of-wedlock pregnancy is paired with a militant anti-abortion stance ("I'm gonna keep my baby"). And in the video for "Open Your Heart," the lecherous men who gaze on Madonna at a peep show are juxtaposed with images of a young boy who mimics her dance moves in a wholly innocent way, and with whom Madonna interacts with playful affection after her shift working in the theater is over. The most overt aspects of these works challenge traditional moral conventions, but the less obvious ones make it simplistic, if not hopelessly prudish, to regard her as purely decadent or obscene.

Nowhere is this dualism more pronounced than in a specifically Catholic context. Crucifixes, for example, were a staple of Madonna's early personal iconography, and one could be alternately irritated, amused, or impressed by the complete lack of self-consciousness in her attitude toward religious symbols. "When I went to Catholic schools, I thought the huge crucifixes nuns wore around their necks with their habits were really beautiful," she said in 1985. "I have one like that now. I wear it sometimes but not onstage. It's too big. It might fly up in the air and hit me in the face." In *Truth or Dare*, she rewards her dancers after a show by handing out rosaries to them, and in one insouciant moment, kisses the feet of a dancer who pleases her. The sheer egotism that animates her psuedo-maternal stance suggests she views herself as a combination of Mary and Jesus rolled into one, and yet the idea that the spirit of both lives in her or anyone else is not exactly contrary to Catholic doctrine. And while one might wish Madonna would show more reverence toward the Church, if she has one iota of uncalculated spontaneity, it would appear that at least a portion of it comes from her religious heritage.

Certainly she seems to think so. Like F. Scott Fitzgerald, and much more than Margaret Mitchell, Madonna is attuned to the sense of immediacy, beauty, and mystery that surrounds Catholicism. But as with them, it casts lingering shadows that she can't quite cast off, as much as she might like to. "Once you're a Catholic, you're always a Catholic—in terms of your feelings of guilt and remorse and whether you've sinned or not," she told *Rolling Stone* magazine in 1989, a remark that has been repeated in different forms throughout her career. "Sometimes I'm wracked with guilt when I needn't be, and that, to me, is left over from my Catholic upbringing. Because in Catholicism you are a born sinner and you are a sinner all your life. No matter how you try and get away with it, the sin is within you all the time."

Andrew Greeley, who has discussed Madonna a number of times in his work, considers the unease she expresses here as both understandable and widespread:

> Anyone who listens to the laity knows how bitter are the revulsions of many against their guilt–dominated Catholic childhood and how many of them claim, like Madonna, that they were taught to believe that anything one enjoys must be wrong. Not all Catholics were educated this way; but if we are honest, we must admit that guilt and anger about that guilt is widespread among Catholics. That most of them cling to their Catholicism (like Madonna) one way or another is evidence that the appeal of Catholic imagery is stronger than the ugliness of Catholic guilt.

"Cling" Madonna did, long after she "left" the Church. In fact, as the 1980s came to a close, it increasingly became the focus of her work.

There's both irony and inevitability to this. Irony, because unlike Jay Gatsby or Scarlett O'Hara, Madonna had achieved her American Dream to a striking degree, attaining a kind of secular grace that very few people experience. Her particular dream was that of the Good Life, and as such had a distinctly late-twentieth-century flavor that might be termed the Dream of Celebrity. The Dream of Celebrity incorporates older versions of the American Dream in that it involves freedom, power, or wealth. But at least as important are physical beauty, grace, *fun*. For celebrities, a work ethic does not mean deferred gratification, but rather gratification through novel and exciting work—work that can be talked about in television shows or gossip columns, work not tethered to a clock the way it is for most of us. Again, it's not as if people like Benjamin Franklin or Andrew Carnegie, who embodied earlier Dreams of Upward Mobility, were not celebrities in their own right, or did not live a life of fame and luxury. Clearly, they did. But neither celebrated—in fact they explicitly condemned—many of the values embodied by the Dream of Celebrity.

Even from the heights of hypocrisy, they did so for good reason: the values inherent in the Dream of Celebrity are a fraud, and we all know it. This is where the inevitability comes in. To put it directly in terms of Madonna: her marriage to Sean Penn was not, as some might magazine editors might have had it, a Hollywood storybook romance; in fact they divorced in 1989. The economic and personal freedom she enjoyed was paid for by a cult of youth and beauty that was not only daunting in its insatiable and increasingly exhausting demands, but which would in any case leave her behind. Of course, that was years away, but even work—which, for many of us, is a refuge that keeps our demons at bay—could pose challenges in this regard. In 1988 Madonna won a prized part in a David Mamet play, *Speed the Plow*, that ran in New York. But the experience proved unexpectedly depressing, as she portrayed a woman who she described as "extremely defeated." To prepare for her role each night, she thought about "things I hadn't dealt with in a long time, things like my mother's death and certain relationships." Though her marriage to Penn was dissolving, their relations were apparently civil enough that Madonna could respond positively to his encouragement that she use this period of personal reflection and relative tumult to inform her music.

The result was the best work of her career.

✳   ✳   ✳

"I'm still hanging on—but I'm doing it wrong."

—*Madonna*, "Promise to Try" (*Like a Prayer*, 1989)

As mentioned at the start of this chapter, *Like a Prayer* is actually three documents: an album, a song, and a video. I think of them as three concentric circles with the video at the center. I say so not only because the video medium is finally the arena of Madonna's greatest strength but also because it is there that the Catholic currents that animate her work are the most obvious and potent. My discussion will thus proceed from the outside in.

In one sense, *Like a Prayer*, the album, is a musical throwback to an earlier era of pop music history in that it could legitimately be called what aficionados call a "concept" album, *i.e.* a collection of discrete but thematically unified songs whose whole is greater than the sum of its parts. Though sometimes assumed to be a product of the rock era—the Beatles' *Sgt. Pepper's Lonely Hearts Club Band* (1967) is the classic example—the real originator of concept album was Frank Sinatra, who in albums like *In the Wee Small Hours* (1955) and *Frank Sinatra Sings for Only the Lonely* (1958) exploited the cultural possibilities inherent in the then-new technology of long–playing vinyl records. The concept album reached its apogee in the 1970s in ambitious records like Pink Floyd's *Dark Side of the Moon* (1973) and The Eagles' *Hotel California* (1977). The introduction of the compact disc in the 1980s (which allowed listeners to program songs in any order they wished), coupled with the advent of MTV, reduced the appeal and prevalence of the concept album, though it never altogether disappeared; indeed, one can discern its presence in hip-hop records like Lauryn Hill's autobiographical song cycle *The Miseducation of Lauryn Hill* (1998).

One of the defining characteristics of the concept album are musical reprises that serve to stitch it together. Thus *Like a Prayer,* which begins with the title track, ends with "Act of Contrition," in which the words of the rite of penance are set to music derived from "Like a Prayer." The mere titles of some of the songs in between— "Till Death Do Us Part," "Promise to Try," "Oh Father"—indicate the degree to which religious practice and ritual suffuse the record.

These strictly musical references are reinforced by others, ranging from the visual iconography of the cover (Madonna's name, capped with a crown and rendered in a baroque style, has a Catholic feel) to the album's dedication "to my mother, who taught me how to pray." In form then, *Like a Prayer* is a concept record; in content, it is a *Catholic* concept record.

I hasten to add that's not *all* it is; as with most concept records, the thematic connections are often loose at best. Thus while the ninth track on the album, "Keep it Together," is a tribute to the power of family and as such is consonant with broader religious themes, the more immediate referent is the music of Sly and the Family Stone, which is clearly being invoked and honored here. The rousing feminist anthem "Express Yourself," which has proven to be one of the more durable songs in Madonna's canon, has no real connection to the main themes at all (though it does to the music of the Staple Singers, a black gospel group). Perhaps not coincidentally, both these songs were co–written with Stephen Bray, while all of the others, with one exception, were co–written with longtime Madonna collaborator Patrick Leonard. (That exception is "Love Song," which Madonna wrote with the prodigiously prolific Prince, who, like Madonna, is known by his first name.) The baroque iconography notwithstanding, the far more obvious allusion on the album cover— which depicts Madonna's exposed midriff and an unsnapped pair of jeans—is to the Rolling Stones' notorious cover for their 1974 album *Sticky Fingers*, which was designed by Andy Warhol, himself a fitfully lapsed Catholic.

Moreover, those songs, with their unmistakable religious orientation, are hardly conventional expressions of piety. Instead, anger, sorrow, and even profanity run riot. "Act of Contrition," for example, is marked by dissonance and barely melodic singing on Madonna's part, degenerating into mock-angry shouting as the word "resolve"—as in "I firmly resolve with the help of thy grace"—seems to prompt, stream-of-consciousness style, the word "reservation," which leads to a diatribe against a hotelier or restaurateur who has no computer record that she even registered. "Till Death Do Us Part" invokes the sanctity of marriage, but the bitterly ironic lyrics depict the disintegration of a relationship with the refrain "He's not in love with her anymore." And "Oh Father," which appears to be addressed to a God-like Silvio Ciccone, repeatedly asserts, "You can't hurt me now."

Ultimately, however, the overarching tone of the record is less strident rejection than a deeply engaged sense of conflict. Initially, the reason the father(s) of "Oh Father" can't hurt the singer is that she fled, but by song's end she's begun to realize that he never wanted to hurt her, and so she imagines a future when she'll be able to accept him, no less than herself, as a victim of larger designs. In "Promise to Try," a guilt- and grief-stricken adult daughter struggles to remember a now-gone mother and her admonitions. And the singer of "Spanish Eyes" asserts that "if there is a Christ, he'll come tonight"—a statement poised on the fulcrum between doubt ("if") and confidence ("he'll come").

The title song, "Like a Prayer," is saturated with ambiguity. When it comes to mixed messages, the key word in Madonna's lexicon is *like*—as in "Like a Virgin," in which the experience described therein feels like that of a woman realizing sexual ecstasy for the very first time. That it's *not* the very first time is utterly apparent, not only from references to previous failed romances, but even more from the cheerful authority with which the singer tells her story: she knows this neighborhood, because she's been here before. A comparable duality marks "Like a Prayer" because what we're talking about here is very *similar* to prayer.

But there are significant differences, too. While the character of "Like a Virgin" speaks from a position of confidence and recognition, the dominant mood of "Like a Prayer" is uncertainty, even fear: this character is disoriented by the mystical experiences she describes—of hearing voices, of falling from the sky, of an unseen power whose childlike presence she discerns at midnight. And while the implicit message of "Like a Virgin" is the assertion "*Not* a Virgin," that of "Like a Prayer" is more like an informed guess: I don't really know how to explain what's happening to me, and the closest I can come to describing it in terms of my prior experience would be to compare it to those times when I've prayed. Confusion, even blind groping, is suggested by further attempts to clarify her experience that also use the word "like": we're told a number of times that it is *like* a dream, that it feels *like* falling, the voice she hears is *like* that of a child or of an angel sighing. These are no coy or clever analogies, but rather expressions of the limits of language to describe forces that are finally beyond human comprehension.

For all the fear, there's also something joyous about "Like a Prayer." It begins with a cacophonous electric guitar that gives way with an abrupt halt as the singer notes that life is a solitary, even lonely, mystery. But the voice she hears calling her name feels like home, an observation that leads to a quickening in the pace of the song, which climaxes in repeated rhyme: "No choice/Your voice can take me there." This is a striking assertion coming from an obvious control freak like Madonna, and suggests the immense appeal of surrender, spiritual or otherwise, for such people. It should be noted, however, that the voice *can*, not *will* take her there, and that she repeatedly talks about her desire, when down on her knees, to take "you" (a lover? God?) to this place of spiritual ecstasy, suggesting both an evangelical impulse to share as well as a lingering desire for control even when she's in a position of relative subordination. Old habits, it appears, die hard.

Far more than anything Madonna sings, it is the choir supporting her, under the direction of Andrae Crouch, that gives the song its expressive power. More than that: it's an important manifestation of its essentially American character. In large measure, this is because such singing is *not* Catholic; instead, it is rooted in the powerful gospel tradition of African American churches. Crouch, a well–known singer, arranger, producer, and evangelical minister, has collaborated with many pop musicians, from Elvis Presley to Michael Jackson, and his work can be heard in such well-known films as *The Lion King* (1994). The gospel tradition he represents is the wellspring of American popular music, and when musicians seek to give their work a particular kind of credibility and power, they access it regularly (think of songs ranging from Aretha Franklin's classic 1968 version of "Respect" to Michael Jackson's 1988 hit "Man in the Mirror," which also features the Andrae Crouch Choir). Madonna is only one of countless white American pop stars who have leaned heavily on black music and black traditions to give their work its vitality.

That vitality is not only musical; it is also moral. Race is the fault line of the American imagination. Our history lacks an Inquisition or a Hitler, but it does have slavery, a brute fact that haunts any effort to think of ourselves as pure. As Abraham Lincoln said during the Civil War, "if slavery is not wrong, then nothing is wrong," and ever since it has been a yardstick by which we have measured ourselves. Even now, with slavery abolished, segregation (theoretically) ended, and when race has long since ceased to be a largely black-and-white affair, it serves as a litmus test of sorts for measuring good and evil.

This racialized vision of morality is central to the video for "Like a Prayer," which represents an unusually thorough integration of African American and Catholic motifs. The most vivid example are the burning crosses that serve as a backdrop for Madonna throughout the video, simultaneously evoking Christ's passion and the Ku Klux Klan—a jarring juxtaposition enlisted in the service of reclaiming the cross from its racist (and anti-Catholic) connotations. The exterior of the church in which Madonna's character finds herself looks somewhat like a rural Baptist church in its simplicity, but its relatively modest interior is laden with flowers, candles, and icons one associates with working-class Latin Catholicism. Dark-haired, voluptuous, and scantily clad, Madonna herself looks like a figure out of a seventeenth-century Spanish painting.

Unlike the album or song, the "Like a Prayer" video has a (silent) story line that accompanies the music. Originally, Madonna thought it would be about an interracial love affair, but she explained that Mary Lambert, who directed the "Like a Virgin" and "Material Girl" videos, among others, "incorporated more of the religious symbolism I originally wrote into the song." In the video, a young woman played by Madonna witnesses a gang assault on a young woman and looks away, apparently in fear. A young black man walking down the street also sees the incident, however, and tries to intervene on the woman's behalf. Just as he does, the police arrive and, assuming he is the perpetrator, arrest him. As they take him away, Madonna's character looks up to see one of the criminals—his chiseled white visage would please Hitler himself—give her a threatening look, as if warning her not to get involved.

Unsure of what to do, she enters a church and sees a figure of a black saint who looks remarkably similar to the man the police arrested. As she kneels to pray, the figure seems to be crying. She lies down and dreams that she is tumbling through the sky. Suddenly she is caught by a black woman in church robes who proceeds to lift her up again. Back inside the church, the saint has come to life; he and Madonna's character kiss in a passionate embrace. Then she picks up a knife that is lying on the ground. Suddenly her hands are bleeding as if she has stigmata. With a black choir now singing ecstatically behind her, the woman, enlivened with new resolve, goes to the local jail, explains what happens to the police, and the innocently accused man is freed.

This summary of the plot makes the video sound a little more straightforward than it really is. For one thing, the action is not always chronological; particular images (like the assault itself, or Madonna dancing in front of the burning crosses) flash forward and back at different points. For another, the line separating dream and reality is not clearly demarcated. In fact, the video has a highly stylized feel that increasingly suspends conventions of realism altogether. Nowhere is this more apparent than the conclusion, where we see Madonna mouth the words "he didn't do it" and the police officer—in a station house whose interior looks similar to the church layout—simply walks over and releases the black man. Of course, the point of this drama is not authenticity; its highly staged, archetypal quality suggests a piece of self-conscious religious pageantry, a quality underlined by the rise and fall of a curtain as the cast takes a bow. In spirit, "Like a Prayer" seems reminiscent of a Catholic school play.

In a 1991 article for the liberation theology-minded *Christianity in Crisis* magazine, writer Mark D. Hulsether deftly characterizes the strengths and weaknesses of the video. Among the strengths, says Hulsether, are that "it sharply rejects racist perversions of Christianity such as the Ku Klux Klan; emphasizes Jesus' human solidarity or identity with the victims of oppression; places the cross in the context of sociopolitical struggle and persecution; and represents the Church as a place of transforming justice." He also notes that it "promotes African American culture and combats both police violence and the scapegoating of black males." Moreover, he adds, "in a way that converges with some feminist theology, it stresses the importance of the erotic for conceptualizing faith." Yet Hulsether argues that "Like a Prayer" "centers too much on Madonna to be a fully satisfying vision of collective empowerment, despite its negative portrayal of sexual violence, stress on interracial solidarity, and heavy emphasis on the black choir." Concluding that the video, like much of Madonna's work—and, for that matter, much American culture generally—is a mixed bag, he argues that the important thing is to sort through it all and find that which is most useful.

Like the characters in *Reservoir Dogs*, we can argue among ourselves just how much value there is here. But if there's one point I hope this discussion makes clear, it is that the Catholic elements that inform "Like a Prayer" specifically and Madonna's work generally are a complex amalgam of conscious choice and unconscious impulse that are anything but accidental or incidental. Even though she acts like a heretic sometimes, and even though her professions of piety are all too often laced with vanity—vanity being a particular pitfall of the American Dream—she remains a child of the Church. In both her lingering attachment and avowed independence, she can help us better understand our own stance toward it, whether we've rejected it or not.

*　*　*

> I think what's important changes for you. For me. Your values change. I know what it's like to be on top and there are great things about it and terrible things about it and I know I can never be in that place and that time again in my life.
>
> —*Madonna, around the time of the release of her 1998 album* Ray of Light

Finally, we can say it: Madonna is history.

Not that *Like a Prayer* was a turning point. Personally, artistically, and commercially, it was a phase in her career she quickly left behind. Madonna again became a platinum blonde, with all that implies, to act and sing in the 1990 film *Dick Tracy*, starring and

directed by then–paramour Warren Beatty. The controversy surrounding "Like a Prayer" seemed mild compared to the firestorm Madonna
ignited by the 1990 song and video "Justify My Love," which was
banned by MTV. And in 1992, Madonna published a book *Sex*, and
an accompanying album, *Erotica*. Both works, which featured graphic
representations of sexual acts, drew even more criticism than "Like
a Prayer" or "Justify My Love" did. By the spring of 1992, she was
as famous as she'd ever been, perhaps even more famous than John
Lennon, who created a worldwide furor in 1966 with an offhand
remark to the London *Evening Standard* that the Beatles were "more
popular than Jesus now." Her Dream of Celebrity seemed to have
limitless horizons.

In retrospect though, *Sex* and *Erotica* were the beginning of
the end of Madonna's moment. After an initial sensation, sales for
both works fizzled, and Madonna herself described the reception of
Erotica as "the biggest disappointment of my career." Perhaps recognizing that her unending quest for novelty was itself becoming
tiresome, she took a more romantic turn in the lush 1994 album
Bedtime Stories (which featured the hits "Secret" and "Take a Bow,"
the latter made into a memorably elegant video involving a Spanish
bullfighter). And she continued to appear in movies, ranging from
her often fascinating, if narcissistic, turn in *Truth or Dare* in 1991 to
her supporting role in *A League of Their Own*, a 1992 film about a
women's softball league during World War II. Her film career reached
its height when she was cast in the much-coveted role of Eva Peron
in *Evita* (1996), for which she won a Golden Globe award in 1997.

Yet all this activity and undeniable success could not quite erase
the impression that Madonna had lost her place on center stage.
New icons of youthful sexuality—the Spice Girls, Jennifer Lopez,
Britney Spears—took the pop music spotlight as the decade
approached its end. Part of this, of course, is generational: Madonna,
who turned forty in 1998, simply could not represent this constitu-
ency the way she did in the early eighties.

Meanwhile, Madonna herself had new priorities. The most
important was children. She bore a daughter, Lourdes, in 1996, to a
man she did not marry, and with whom her relationship did not
continue long after the child's birth; and a son with film director

Guy Ritchie, whom she married in 2000 shortly after the child was born. Her 1998 album *Ray of Light* reflected her restless search for novelty in its sound (which drew on the then-current ambient/techno style embraced by the glitterati); its subjects (many of the songs were about motherhood); and its religious themes (a smorgasbord that included Hindu and mystical Jewish as well as conventional Christian elements: as with other aspects of her life, it appears Madonna has trouble making sustained religious commitments). The album was respectfully reviewed and the title track in particular spawned a much played and admired video, but it was not the blockbuster that *Like a Virgin* or *Like a Prayer* had been. The release of her album *Music* in 2000 was similarly received. "I may not be as popular as I once was, but people are starting to pay attention to my music and respect me as an artist more," she said in a rare moment of retrospective candor. That she has earned lasting fame, even affection, seems likely. But it's her videos more than her music that are likely to prove durable, and she is more likely to be remembered as a vivid embodiment of her era than as an artist, like F. Scott Fitzgerald or Margaret Mitchell, whose creations long outlived their times.

We don't know, of course, what will finally become of Madonna. Perhaps she will come roaring back, whether as a nostalgia act or by blazing a path on the baby-booming frontier of sex for seniors. Maybe her Catholicism, which went into marked retreat after *Like a Prayer*, will again resurface and give her work the power and intensity it had at that pivotal moment.

But even if nothing more of note happens, Madonna's career highlights a crucial transition in the history of Catholicism and the American Dream. For F. Scott Fitzgerald and Margaret Mitchell, the Church was somehow a wrinkle in their identities, a potentially unsettling difference between their characters and the rest of their society to be at best tolerated by themselves and others. Yet whatever her problems with the Church, Madonna has never suggested her religion was anything she had to hide, ignore, apologize for, or— perhaps most tellingly of all—protect in her pursuit of the American Dream. She has both worn her Catholicism and discarded it with the sense of confidence of a post-Kennedy generation for whom religious affiliation was no more an issue than eye or hair color, inherited features whose appearance could be manipulated or changed at will.

Is this progress? In at least one sense, it certainly is. The sense of freedom Madonna and other Americans enjoy is a direct result of the cultural logic of Protestantism, in which the choice of the individual conscience is regarded as the highest of values even for those of other religious traditions, and in which choice is rhetorically enshrined (if not always actually honored) in every other aspect of American life, most notably consumer culture. That the choices we and others make are not uniformly attractive should not blind us to the tremendous benefits of such a society, especially compared with the avowedly coercive ones of the past and present and the sins that can result. At the same time, however, American Catholics are one of those peoples (Jews are another) who have had the historical experience of inhabiting sacred identities that could not be chosen coupled with secular identities that could. This particular form of double consciousness, as difficult and painful as it can be to live with, is nevertheless still of value. Sometimes, *not* choosing—or to put in more American terms, choosing to accept the weight of history, religious and otherwise—can be the most satisfying form of freedom. It can afford a sense of grounding in a society where seemingly limitless choices can produce grinding fatigue, if not anxiety, or even a sense of loss.

To judge on the basis of her work since *Like a Prayer,* Madonna does not agree. But other Catholics, including a fellow Italian American with a similarly checkered religious history, has taken this idea seriously. It is to him, and our final case study in this book, that we now turn.

STANDING BY JESUS

Willem Dafoe and Martin Scorsese in a publicity still for the 1988 film *The Last Temptation of Christ*. Though criticized by conservative Christians as a willful work of apostasy, *Temptation* was a sincere ecumenical affirmation of Christ's human dimensions, one filtered through director Scorsese's urban Italian-American Catholic childhood. *(Photo courtesy of The Kobal Collection, New York)*

Chapter Six

IT'S A WONDERFUL DEATH:
THE CASE OF (MARTIN SCORSESE'S) JESUS CHRIST

> *To a filmwise viewer, the cumulative effect of all this resembles nothing so much as an inverted variation on Frank Capra's* It's a Wonderful Life.
>
> —from the review of Martin Scorsese's
> *The Last Temptation of Christ* in *Variety*,
> a Hollywood trade newspaper, August 1988

For a long time, I avoided *It's a Wonderful Life*. In some ways, this was hard to do: though not a great favorite at the time of its release in 1946 (the film failed to earn back its costs at the box office, and while it was nominated for a number of major Academy Awards, it did not win any), it has become a kind of sacred scripture in the world of American popular culture, a longtime staple of Christmastime television broadcasts, a fixture at video stores, and a kind of common cultural shorthand—you've no doubt read a newspaper columnist or heard a neighbor say something like "it's something right out of *It's a Wonderful Life*." At a time when even a film like *Gone with the Wind* seems to have receded somewhat in the seemingly ever more youth–minded collective consciousness, *Life* seems to be holding its own.

There are a number of reasons for *Life*'s durability. They include the quality of the writing, acting, and directing, as well as a lapse in the film's copyright—hence all those Christmas Eve broadcasts, for which television stations did not have to pay for the rights. But a major factor in *Life*'s appeal is its function as an exceptionally vivid document in the history of the American Dream. In the story of George Bailey (Jimmy Stewart), an earnest young man who desperately wants to, but never quite escapes, the small town of Bedford Falls, the viewer witnesses a virtual compendium of Dreams—education, travel, military heroism, capitalist enterprise, and more. Yet they all somehow pass George by, as one set of circumstances after another (like a run on banks during the Great Depression) force him to remain in town to run the family savings and loan business. In a moment of profound crisis he seriously considers suicide. But the intervention of his guardian angel, who allows him to see what would have happened had he never lived, allows him to recognize the preciousness of a life that is in many respects a dream come true.

Hokey plot devices (such as the guardian angel) led many critics at the time of its release and long after to dismiss *It's a Wonderful Life* as mawkish tripe that typified the work of Frank Capra, the Italian Catholic immigrant who directed it—his movies, which included *Mr. Smith Goes to Washington* (1939) and *Meet John Doe* (1941), were sometimes dismissed as "Capracorn." But that's not why I avoided the movie. If you had pressed me, I might have told you that it had something to do with the film being shot in black and white; a child of color, I've always found something dated, even oppressive, about old movies. That's an attitude I outgrew. But even after I had actually seen *It's a Wonderful Life* all the way through— and assigned it for a course I taught on the American Dream—I still find it hard to watch. It's a scary, even creepy, movie.

To a great extent, this is by design. The syrupy elements in *It's a Wonderful Life* don't quite balance the sour, even bitter, ones. In fact, they may even enhance their impact. It's precisely because Jimmy Stewart—whose associations as a Good Guy resonate far beyond his portrayal of George Bailey—is such a seemingly sane and responsible character that his unraveling is all the more unnerving (I can never forget the first time I saw the feverish look in his eyes as he prepares to jump off a bridge in the middle of a snowstorm). When, in a moment anxiety and despair, he responds to his pestering children by angrily posing a rhetorical question to his wife Mary (Donna Reed) about why they ever even *had* children, I watch amazed at the frankness of his resentment. Even presumably "good" moments—and there are many in the movie—are tinged with pain (we know from the start, after all, that George is headed for a crisis). A good example of this is when George, as a child working for the neighborhood pharmacist Mr. Gower, does not deliver a prescription because he knows that Mr. Gower, who was drunk when he filled it, inadvertently used poison instead of medicine. Upon George's return to the store, an angry Gower assaults the boy, hitting him on the ear that George damaged a few years earlier when he saved his brother Harry from drowning. When Gower finally realizes that George has saved him, too, he collapses to his knees in gratitude ("I know you didn't mean it!" says a crying George, who even as a child has the compassion to recognize that Gower's grief over the loss of his son in the influenza epidemic of 1919 has led to his drinking). Stewart and Capra are responsible for giving such wrenching scenes their tremendous affective power.

Yet it may well be the unintentional implications of *It's a Wonderful Life* that finally prove most disturbing. This is especially true of the ending. To be sure, there's a great deal that's reassuring about it: after seeing just how much a difference he has made in the lives of the people around him, George returns to his own life with a new appreciation, and the denizens of Bedford Falls pull together to replace the $8000 his Uncle Billy lost to the machinations of the evil Henry Potter (played with great verve by Lionel Barrymore). The dashing Harry Bailey's heartfelt toast to his brother—"the richest man in Bedford Falls"—is meant partly as a joke, but more importantly as tribute to the genuine resources and accomplishments of the stay-at-home George. And the presence of his guardian angel as a light atop the Bailey Christmas tree represents the final form of affirmation at the scene. Yet none of this can erase the film's darker realities: that Potter has gone unpunished for his sins; that friendship is literally a matter of money; and, perhaps most disturbingly, that it is unmistakably evident that George Bailey will never realize his youthful dreams, at best exchanging them for a fragile vision of domesticity that was his wife's much more than his.

Film historian Robert Ray, who notes these and other discordant elements, put his finger on just why I have always found this movie so haunting. "George experienced the movie's most pessimistic truth, that the value attached to even our most cherished objects—Christmas, home, marriage, family, life itself—rested on the thinnest tissue of sustaining faith that could be torn by the most random of accidents (such as Uncle Billy's loss of the deposit funds)," he writes. "Without that faith, even these cherished things became nightmarish." Ray concludes that "It is this glimpse of the utter emptiness of American life that remained despite the film's happy ending . . . Only the will to keep believing in the traditional pattern of reconciliation made *It's a Wonderful Life* into at least a superficially optimistic story. That almost everyone cried at the end suggested the audience's sense of how narrow the escape had been for that pattern and the faith behind it." Celebrated as quintessential document—and affirmation—of the American Dream, *It's a Wonderful Life* nevertheless raises questions that can be troubling to those of us with an investment in it.

I make these remarks about an old Hollywood movie as a prelude to talking about a much newer Hollywood movie, also by a Italian-American Catholic director, that I similarly avoided for a long time after I was aware of it: Martin Scorsese's 1988 film *The Last Temptation of Christ*, based on the 1951 novel by Nikos Kazantzakis, the famed Greek writer best known for his 1943 novel *Zorba the Greek*. As a reviewer from *Variety* noted in passing, *Last Temptation* is an inversion of *Life*. While the latter depicts what would have happened if its protagonist did not *live*, the former shows what would have happened if its protagonist did not *die*: in this telling, a long, largely happy life that included many children by three different women. Like *Life*, *Temptation* had its critics, but here too there was a kind of inversion. While *Life* was attacked by secular liberals impatient with its tolerance of capitalism, *Temptation* was attacked by fundamentalist evangelicals, who called it "an intentional attack on Christianity" and deplored what they regarded as "the urge to assault the cherished recollections of even universally esteemed figures in our culture." The furor surrounding *Temptation*, which included protests at movie theaters and some ugly accusations that it was a Jewish attempt to discredit Christianity on the part of Hollywood mogul Lew Wasserman, ebbed relatively quickly, and at least one conservative Christian has expressed regret that the film was ever the focus of evangelical ire.

The concerns of such people were not, in any event, the reason I avoided the movie. I did so for the same reason I avoided *Life*: fear. If Frank Capra's movie suggested to me that the American Dream is fragile and perhaps unrealizable, at some unarticulated level I suspected Martin Scorsese's film would show it to be an illegitimate and even dangerous faith.

Those fears have some justification. But there's more to the movie than that. Indeed, while *Temptation* is not necessarily a great film—in fact, it might not even be a great Martin Scorsese film—it is nevertheless a deeply revealing document of its time and place, and dramatizes important aspects of the American Dream in Catholic culture. And so I'd like to make my final case study an exploration of one particular portrait of a man who cannot help but be of consequence to anyone with a belief in the American Dream. That man—and it's important to note that whatever else may be true, we *are* talking about a *man* here—is Jesus Christ.

✳   ✳   ✳

I made it as a prayer, an act of worship. I wanted to be a priest. My whole life has been movies and religion. That's it. Nothing else.

—*Martin Scorsese on* The Last Temptation of Christ

In its origins, *The Last Temptation of Christ* is an unusually catholic document, and as the lower case "c" suggests, I mean this in an ecumenical, not sectarian, sense. Nikos Kazantzakis, who wrote the novel that became the basis of the movie, belonged (in his inconstant way) to the Greek Orthodox Church. Paul Schrader, who wrote the first draft screenplay for the film, grew up (and rebelled against) his Dutch Reformed congregation in Grand Rapids, Michigan. And Martin Scorsese, who directed *Temptation*, has described himself as "a devout Catholic, even if I'm not a 'good' Catholic." While these three strains of Christianity are clearly present in the movie—and there are a number of elements in the film, notably its music, costumes, and settings, that have decisively Hebrew and even Arab flavors—the Catholic accents are of special interest for this particular discussion, and will thus be our focus here.

To a great extent, that means focusing on Scorsese. While one suspects that aspects of his childhood in New York's Little Italy have been exaggerated, even mythologized, through frequent retellings, there can be little question that his ethnicity and religion were absolutely central to the formation of his artistic vision.

Martin Scorsese was born in Queens, New York on November 17, 1942, the youngest of two sons. Scorsese's mother, Catherine, had been born in Sicily; his father, Charles, was born in Little Italy, a neighborhood in the lower east side of Manhattan, shortly after his parents had left Sicily. Both parents were skilled workers in the garment industry, and in some ways were relatively prosperous (the family was the first one on the block, for instance, to own a television set, which they bought principally for young Martin's benefit). But financial setbacks led Charles Scorsese to move his family back to his father's apartment in Little Italy, directly across from his in-laws. After several months, he found another apartment a few doors down, and Martin spent the rest of his childhood there.

That childhood was a highly confined one. Young Scorsese was asthmatic, which limited his engagement with the outside world, and the neighborhood itself was a post-World War II holdout in the rapidly disappearing world of immigrant solidarity and isolation. "Elizabeth Street [where he lived] was mainly Sicilian, as were my grandparents, and here the people had their own regulations and laws," he later explained. "We didn't care about the government, or politicians, or the police: we felt we were right in our ways." Those ways included looking the other way when ordered to do so by the *capos* who organized and ran the neighborhood.

Scorsese had two major avenues to the world beyond Little Italy. The first was the Roman Catholic Church, which meant more to him than it did his parents. "I don't think the Church figured into their life very much," he told film critic Richard Corliss in 1988. They were "Italian Italian [as opposed to Italian American] Catholics, like my assistant Rafael Donato, who says 'We're really pagans. Pagans in the good sense. We enjoy life, we put the church in a certain perspective.' My parents were able to do that."

Young Martin, however, was not. For him the Church was a far more mesmerizing force, one that had a deeply mystical—and visual—power. "The first images I recall were the plaster statues and crucifixes in St. Patrick's Old Cathedral," he recalled of his parish church. "The strongest impression was of a human being who had been tortured and beaten, then put on the cross, and this was someone you would have loved, who had been a very good person. I remember being taken to a Mass and wondering why my parents had never taken me before. It was so impressive, with different colored vestments for the different Masses: white and gold, or green and gold."

These were not fleeting impressions, and Scorsese's involvement in the Church for much of his youth was fairly intense. "My friends used to say, 'Jeeze, Marty, do you really *believe* all that stuff the priests tell you?' Well, I did believe it, every word of it. I wouldn't touch meat on Friday, and I believed I would go to hell if I missed Mass on Sunday." Scorsese, who attended Catholic school and served as an altar boy, had an especially strong affinity for Catholic ritual, as he suggests in this description of his childhood religious practice:

For me, Holy Week was always a very powerful time, even more dramatic than Christmas. The rituals were dramatic. The liturgies were beautiful. The Stations of the Cross were very dramatic. This colored my whole sense of God. I preferred Christmas, as I guess everyone does, because you get gifts, and it's more fun. It's a happy time. But in Holy Week, you have to go through Spy Wednesday, Holy Thursday, Good Friday, and Holy Saturday to reach Easter Sunday. The names alone are dramatic. It's called Passion Week. It's a scary time. But it's exhilarating, too, and very beautiful.

In formal terms, the culmination of this sense of religious engagement occurred when Scorsese was fourteen, and his parents sent him to a junior seminary on Manhattan's West Side, the first step in the process whereby one becomes a priest. "I thought a lot about salvation," he said, "and it seemed that the best guarantee of being saved was to be a priest, which would be like being able to pick up the phone any time and talk to God."

Ultimately, however, this proved to be the high watermark of Scorsese's institutional engagement with the Church. The reasons are not altogether clear; his parents spoke of his failure to learn Latin at the junior seminary, while Scorsese himself speaks of misadventure and the charm of girls and rock and roll. But most fundamentally, he found himself unable to close the gap between the world inside church walls and the one outside it. "To take religion like that seriously, and then to hit those streets that are full of lawlessness, is another story," he explained. "You want to know how to combine it and try to put the two together. It's impossible. And this is just a microcosm of the world, isn't it?"

As he grew up, it became increasingly clear that Scorsese's efforts to perform the impossible coalesced around the other great passion of his youth: cinema. The sickly child was taken to the movies frequently by his father and older brother, and the presence of a television in his home gave him plenty to watch on his solitary days. Scorsese loved Westerns, but he also loved foreign films too, which he saw frequently because Hollywood hostility toward the new medium meant that broadcasters had to look farther afield for early television broadcasting. Thus Scorsese got plenty of Roberto Rossellini along with John Wayne, laying the foundations for an unusually rich imaginative framework from which his own deeply personal vision would emerge.

Despite his growing estrangement from the Church, religion remained very much a part of that vision. "I always wanted to make a film of the life of Christ, ever since I saw him portrayed on the screen in *The Robe* when I was eleven years old," Scorsese remembered of the 1953 biblical epic. "I was an altar boy, and I was taken by our diocesan priest on a little field trip up to the Roxy. He hated the film for its absurdity, but I'll never forget the magic of walking down the lobby and getting a glimpse of that gigantic CinemaScope screen for the first time. And when I heard the music in stereophonic sound, it became confused in my mind with the Gregorian Chant for the Mass of the Dead, at which I used to serve every Saturday morning at 10:30."

In 1960 Scorsese enrolled at New York University, which at the time was mostly a local institution for upwardly mobile working-class students not attending schools, like Fordham or Baruch, with religious affiliations. Literally speaking, NYU was a short walk away from Scorsese's neighborhood, but figuratively, the highly secular, bohemian air of the place (this, after all, was young Bob Dylan's stomping ground) was much further. Nevertheless, Scorsese, who majored in film studies, took his religious obsessions along with him. In fact his very first movie treatment, or synopsis, was titled *Jerusalem, Jerusalem,* and called for episodes from the Gospels shot in contemporary settings—a Cana-like wedding feast in a tenement, for example, or Jesus being beaten by police and dragged through jeering crowds on the streets of New York. The treatment was never made into a film, but was part of a planned trilogy, whose third part, after some false starts and successfully realized short films, culminated in his first major feature, *Mean Streets,* which he co–wrote, directed, and acted in (as an assassin).

In Scorsese's words, "*Mean Streets* dealt with the American Dream, according to which everybody thinks they can get rich quick, and if they can't do it by legal means, then they'll do it by illegal ones." But while a film like Francis Ford Coppola's *The Godfather* (1972) tells this story with gangsters on an epic scale, *Mean Streets* looks at comparatively small-time crooks, people whose lives are tightly centered in the ethnic enclave of Little Italy. The movie tells the story of Charlie Cappa (Harvey Keitel), an upwardly mobile junior mafioso who works for his Uncle Giovanni (Cesare Danova) and who stands to take over a restaurant whose owner is unable to pay his debts. Charlie is in love with Theresa (Amy Robinson), an epileptic woman in the neighborhood, and feels a deep sense of obligation to her wild cousin, Johnny Boy (Robert De Niro), neither of whom his uncle approves. Johnny Boy is dangerously indebted to a loan shark (Richard Romanus), and Charlie tries to intervene on Johnny Boy's behalf, but Johnny Boy's reckless behavior only makes matters worse. In a desperate move to escape the conflicts that surround him, Charlie tries to take Johnny Boy and Theresa away from their problems, but the three get no farther than the Brooklyn Bridge before they are engulfed by violence.

Mean Streets is indeed about the simultaneously specific and inchoate aspirations that define the American Dream, but the dramatic power of this theme comes from the friction provided by Roman Catholicism, which is an even more obvious and potent element in the story. This friction is apparent right from the opening lines of dialogue, which the viewer hears before an image is even shown: "You don't make up for sins in church. You do it in the streets. The rest is bullshit and you know it." We then see Charlie in a church (Old St. Patrick's Cathedral, Scorsese's own parish church), and it becomes obvious as the story proceeds that he views Johnny Boy as his pet moral project. One problem Charlie has, however, is that Johnny doesn't particularly *want* a guardian angel—unless Charlie is willing to turn to his uncle for help, something Charlie resolutely refuses to do. More important, Charlie fails to recognize (as Johnny seems to) that Charlie's efforts, even his seemingly selfless ones, are really more for his own spiritual benefit. "Charlie uses other people, thinking that he's helping them," Scorsese once explained. "But by believing that, he's not only ruining them, he's ruining himself."

Frank Principe, a parish priest in Scorsese's neighborhood during his childhood, has aptly described the vein of Italian Catholicism that courses through Scorsese's body of work:

> Marty Scorsese was very intelligent and intense, and with a very, very, good sense of humor. He was incarnational in his approach to religion; he was able to find God in things. To him, as to most Italians, religion is incarnational, earthy. The worst sins are not of the flesh but rather *superba*, or pride. The sins of the flesh are signs of human weakness. But pride, putting man in God's place, that was very serious because it's a direct rejection of God.

Many of the things Principe talks about here—Scorsese's intelligence, intensity and humor; his incarnational approach to religion (typified, for example, by the presence of literal or figurative crosses or crucifixes); and above all his exploration of the sin of pride—are hallmarks of his movies. Indeed, while he would go on to make a striking variety of films, from the female–centered world of *Alice Doesn't Live Here Anymore* (1975) to the remote milieu of the Dalai Lama in *Kundun* (1998), they are unified by a common set of ideas that revolve around the struggles of outsiders to first determine, and than live out, a morally acceptable and satisfying vision of life without succumbing to despair or hubris.

Usually, though, when one thinks of a Martin Scorsese film, the first images that come to mind are not those of, say, his meticulously observed adaptation of Edith Wharton's *The Age of Innocence* (1993), but rather a remarkable string of movies that explore the cultural framework from which he sprang: *Mean Streets* in 1973, *Taxi Driver* in 1976, and *Raging Bull* in 1980. These films, supplemented by *Goodfellas* in 1990 and *Casino* in 1995, are unified by a number of elements: the obsessive personalities of their characters (e.g., Charlie's irrational fixation with Johnny Boy); the barely concealed rage that can erupt into violence at any moment (the frighteningly powerful and resilient boxer Jake LaMotta of *Raging Bull*, embodied unforgettably by De Niro); and an often savage sense of irony (as when, in *Taxi Driver*, the deeply troubled would-be presidential assassin, again played by De Niro, ends up a media hero for his blood-soaked "rescue" of the child prostitute played by Jodie Foster, in a role that "inspired" real-life would-be assassin John Hinckley to shoot Ronald Reagan in 1981).

By the time of the release of *Raging Bull* in 1980, Scorsese had established himself as one of the premier directors of his generation, one that included Coppola, Steven Spielberg, and George Lucas. And yet, while Scorsese was very much in the world of big–budget Hollywood filmmaking, he was never quite of it in the way of his peers. Many of his movies have performed respectably at the box office, but he's never had a blockbuster on the scale of *The Godfather*, *E.T.*, or *Star Wars*. Nor has he ever won an Academy Award—an oversight that says far more about the provincialism of American movie culture than it does about Scorsese. For much of his career, he has had to proceed without the certainty that he would continue to *have* a career, and budgetary limitations have been pervasive enough that he has been forced to use them as a spur to greater creativity (Scorsese has often cited a lack of time and money as a principal influence on the striking look and sound of *Mean Streets*, which was shot in a mere twenty-seven days without any constructed sets). It was this dual prospect of achievement and adversity that faced

Scorsese when, in the early 1980s, he embarked on a project he had been planning for many years: a film adaptation of *The Last Temptation of Christ.*

＊　＊　＊

"I realized that he had been preparing for this film his whole life . . . I don't think Marty can help it; there's nothing else he can do with his life."

—*Barbara Hershey, who plays Mary Magdalene in* The Last Temptation of Christ, *on Scorsese's vocation*

The Last Temptation of Christ had a troubled history long before Scorsese came along. The author of the novel, Nikos Kazantzakis, wrote the book toward the end of a long life that included forays into Communism, Buddhism, and immersion in the work of philosophers Henri Bergson and Friedrich Nietzche. His 1952 book *The Greek Passion* brought him close to excommunication, and upon his death in 1957, the Orthodox Greek archbishop refused to allow his body to lie in state in a church (he was granted a Christian burial in his birthplace of Crete). *The Last Temptation of Christ* was placed on the Papal Index of forbidden books in 1954, three years after its publication in Greek.

Why all the furor, then and later? Many objected to the mere premise of Jesus as a sexually active man, a scenario that unfolds at the end of the story, and which became the focus of conservative Christian protest when the movie was released in 1988. Such a premise is indeed sensationalistic, as is the scene where Jesus watches while a roomful of customers wait to have sex with Mary Magdalene, though a look at how either the book or the film handled these scenes would reveal them to be much less lurid than critics (many of whom neither read the book nor saw the movie) contended. Still, there is little question that there is much to *Temptation* that is indeed objectionable on theological grounds across many Christian denominations.

The heart of the problem lay in the way Kazantzakis's novel

plunged headlong into an issue that has animated Christianity at least since the First Council of Nicaea in A.D. 325: the question of whether Jesus Christ was God or man. The answer, then and ever since, has been both, but at different times in different communities one aspect or the other has been emphasized. Kazantzakis's insistent view of Jesus Christ as a fully human figure who only gradually—and with great difficulty—came to understand and fulfill his divine destiny was meant to be a corrective to what he and others regarded as a moribund tendency to exalt (and thus distance) him. Critics of Kazantzakis, and later Scorsese, argued that both went much too far in portraying Christ with a prolonged identity crisis, and perhaps even more importantly that their human emphasis came dangerously close to conflating human importance with that of God. This was something that Paul Schrader, a screenwriter with an unusually sure grasp of theology, acknowledged. "When critics of the film accuse it of blasphemy, they are right in a way, they are right in a highly intellectual level, not at a visceral, superficial level," he has said. "To use Jesus Christ as a character, as a metaphor for the human condition, is technically a form of blasphemy since as God, how can he [Christ] be a metaphor for man?" This too is a question with a long history, dating back to the Council of Chalcedon in 451, which allowed the representation of Christ in art. The decision was reaffirmed in the Second Council of Nicaea in 787, but there has been a persistent Christian tradition, running from the Iconoclasts through the Puritans, that has questioned the legitimacy of human representations of God in anything approaching a realistic form. This realism—what Father Principe called an "incarnational" sensibility—is precisely what appealed to Scorsese, whose visual orientation was a combination of his religious heritage as well as his cinematic training.

Another significant aspect of Kazantzakis's work, one part of his worldview long before he wrote *Temptation*, was his anti-institutional stance toward organized religion. "He was not primarily interested in reinterpreting Christ or in disagreeing with, or reforming, the Church," translator P. A. Bien wrote in an afterword to the English edition of the novel. "He wanted, rather, to lift Christ out of the church altogether, and—since in the twentieth century the old era was dead or dying—to rise to the occasion and exercise man's right (and duty) to fashion a new saviour and thus rescue himself from a moral and spiritual void." Such an approach closely paralleled that of Scorsese, whose Catholicism lapsed as a formal matter but which remained a forceful presence in movies like *Mean Streets*. "My feeling is that if you were to take yourself to the point where there are no churches, just you alone with God, that's the plane on which I wanted to make the film," he said of *Temptation*. (In the emphasis on the individual and God, there's something recognizably Protestant about such a sentiment, suggesting the American overlay to Scorsese's Catholicism.)

None of this is meant to suggest that Scorsese himself approached the making of *Temptation* with anything like an academic appreciation of the theological issues or even a clear plan on how to proceed. Indeed, in reviewing the history of the making of the film, little is more striking than on just how gradual and intermittent his attention was to the project. Scorsese had heard of the book as early as 1961, when a Greek friend at NYU brought it to his attention. But he didn't actually begin reading the novel until 1972, when it was given to him by actor Barbara Hershey, who would eventually play the role of Mary Magdalene. In 1977 he optioned the rights to the novel and entrusted the writing of a screenplay to Schrader, who didn't actually complete a script until 1982. In early 1983 Paramount Pictures agreed to finance the movie, and with the approval of Kazantzakis's widow, Scorsese began scouting locations in Israel, where the film was to be shot. Sets were constructed and actors cast (De Niro had no interest in playing Jesus, and the part originally went to Aidan Quinn).

Then things started to go wrong. As often happens, production costs began to rise, making studio executives nervous. More serious was a letter-writing campaign started by a group of women called the Evangelical Sisterhood, which resulted in five hundred letters of protest a day arriving at Gulf + Western, which owned Paramount at the time. The studio made some effort to respond to these concerns, going so far as to host a theological seminar attended by Catholic and Protestant theologians. But when the head of the United Artists theater chain, the second largest in the country, announced it would not show the film, the project was politically and financially crippled. By the end of 1983, Paramount had pulled the plug. For a while, it looked like financing might come from the French government, whose arts ministry was committed to supporting the work of artists of international standing, but similar protests there killed that prospect.

Scorsese, who had courted physical and emotional breakdown in the years preceding the project, struggled to regain his balance in the aftermath of *Temptation*'s cancellation. He did so by taking on two projects, *After Hours* (1985) and *The Color of Money* (1986) that were less a matter of deep personal engagement, as all his previous movies had been, than an effort to succeed as a conventional journeyman director. The latter in particular was a solid financial success, and with an implicit promise to do more of this (which he did in the 1991 film *Cape Fear*), Scorsese, now represented by the powerful Hollywood agent Michael Ovitz, secured financing for *Temptation* from Universal Studios. A number of previously engaged collaborators—notably Schrader and Quinn—were no longer available. They were replaced by Scorsese's longtime friend (and *Time* reviewer) Jay Cocks, who worked with Scorsese to revise the script, and Willem Dafoe, who took the part of Jesus.

Though Scorsese and Cocks made numerous changes as the project went into production again in 1987, Schrader's work remained the core text from which they worked. That text greatly streamlined Kazantzakis's novel, as even a long (over two and one-half hours) movie must condense any five-hundred-page book, but retained the novelist's focus on three core characters: Jesus, Mary Magdalene, and Judas Iscariot. Kazantakis's conceit in the novel was that Mary Magdalene had become a prostitute in frustration over Jesus' failure to marry her despite their powerful love for each other from the time they were children. Judas, whom Jesus has also apparently known for a long time, is highly active in a secret Israelite insurrectionary movement to overthrow Roman rule. At first he intends to murder Jesus, who in a willful attempt to reject others' expectations of him, is employed at the start of the novel as a carpenter who makes crucifixes for the occupying Romans. But Judas begins to suspect that Jesus may in fact be the Messiah, and he suspends his plan, ultimately becoming the most important apostle. Far from a traitor who betrays Christ out of greed, Judas is instead the man to whom Jesus entrusts the agonizing burden of turning him over to his enemies so that the Scriptures could be fulfilled.

This is, however, getting ahead of the story (which, aside from some relatively minor plot details or cinematic devices, follows the same basic trajectory in both book and film).[10] Even when Jesus decides not to resist what seems to be his calling, he is dogged by uncertainty about what God really wants from him and whether he can deliver. He goes to a monastery to dedicate himself to the Lord, but learns that his destiny is to go out among the people. Yet, even with this much direction, he proves tentative, hoping that he can "just open my mouth and let God do the talking." His first major address in the film, a variation on the Sermon on the Mount, shows Jesus stirring a small crowd of followers, only to have them disperse as a bloodthirsty mob when his emphasis on love for the poor is interpreted as a call for death to the rich.

Jesus begins building a following—in a graceful montage, Scorsese shows it growing from a small band of apostles to a considerably larger one—but he remains uncertain. He sees John the Baptist, who counsels him to make a pilgrimage to the desert. There Jesus confronts and overcomes a series of temptations—a seductive snake that speaks to him in the voice of Mary Magdalene; a lion who speaks to him in the voice of Judas; a Satanic flame that warns him that his temptations are not yet over—and comes back to his flock with a newly toughened sense of confidence, even aggressiveness, about his vocation (where before he spoke of love, he now speaks of the ax with which he will remove dead spiritual wood). In the days that follow, we see a Jesus increasingly comfortable in his role, able to enjoy himself at Cana, to withstand his rejection by his own people in Nazareth, and in performing miracles that spread his message across Judea.

Yet even when his earthly stature is at its zenith, Jesus is startled by his own power. Scorsese dramatizes this sense of awe vividly in his depiction of the raising of Lazarus, in which he conveys the experience —through the keening sounds of mourners; the attempts of the crowd to avoid the smell as the tombstone is rolled away; and in the sheer terror in Jesus' eyes as Lazurus's hand suddenly extends out of the darkness—in a way a novel never can. These scenes are augmented by other elements, such as the striking Moroccan landscape and Peter Gabriel's evocatively eclectic soundtrack, that give the film a small-scale immediacy, a bracing contrast with previous generations of biblical epics.

The story moves toward its climax in relatively rapid order as Jesus throws the moneychangers out of the Temple, holds the Last Supper, gets arrested, is interrogated by Pontius Pilate (played in a key of silky indifference by David Bowie), and is crucified. Once on the cross, though, something unexpected happens: an angel comes and tells Jesus his work is finished. Just as Abraham did not actually have to sacrifice Isaac, so too the Son of Man need not actually be killed, either. Better than that: he can and does finally marry Mary Magdalene. When, pregnant with his child, Mary is suddenly taken from him, Jesus follows the guidance of his angel and goes to live with Lazarus's sisters Mary and Martha, both of whom bear him children. Christianity goes on without him—Saul becomes Paul, and spreads the Good News regardless of what actually happened on that cross (or Jesus's own wishes in the matter)—and Jesus lives to see the destruction of the Temple by the Romans in A.D. 70. It's at this point that he receives a visit from the apostles, led by Judas, who chastise him for failing to fulfill the original plan. Suddenly realizing that the guardian angel is in fact Satan, Jesus begs for God's forgiveness for succumbing to this final temptation of a good life and asks to return to the cross. As it turns out, this whole post-resurrection life has been a dream, and in awakening from it and embracing his death, Jesus finally completes his transformation into the Savior whose resurrection will transform the world.

Given this brief plot summary of the movie, one might wonder what, if anything, reflects Scorsese's specifically Catholic obsessions and how they worked themselves into the movie. The answer, in terms of plot, is very little. But when one looks closely at the overall thrust of the story, and explores some very specific choices the director made, one can discern a clear "Romanization" of *Temptation*.

Once again, Schrader is an excellent source of explanation. In his audio commentary accompanying the DVD version of the movie, the screenwriter says that Kazantzakis's vision of Christianity fused

Eastern and Western philosophical traditions. From the East he drew on an emphasis on collective consciousness; from the West a Nietzchean emphasis on the individual quest. Schrader noted that those who complained the film's clear Western bias had "a fair objection," though he considers that bias an understandable one given the perspective of the filmmakers and the audience for the movie. In any event, *Temptation* places far more emphasis on the travails of one man than in emphasizing the degree to which his life and death is a merging of the world's souls.

Of course, to be Western is not necessarily to be Catholic. In fact, Schrader believes that in the element of speculation that animates the novel, i.e., its attempt to affirm the necessity of Christ's death and resurrection by contemplating the implications of an alternative scenario, *Temptation* has special appeal for the Protestant imagination. Certainly he felt it did within the context of his own Dutch Reformed background, which he describes as "essentially a kind of thinker's religion." Calvin, Schrader says, "sort of believed you can think your way into heaven, and therefore reduced faith to a pinhole and constructed a wall of logic around it, the fallacy in this being that a pinhole of faith is the same size as a barn door."

In the end, however, the filmmakers tipped the scales in a decisively Catholic direction. "In Marty Scorsese's urban, Roman Catholic view, much more weight was given to the imagistic, the emotional, and the impressionistic aspects of Catholicism—the iconography, the candles, the ritual," he explains. How was this done? One example is a rare scene that Schrader wrote that was *not* derived from the book, in which Jesus returns from the desert and tries to unify and enlighten his querulous disciples. He does this by pulling his heart out of his chest, stunning them into silence. This depiction of a sacred heart, right down to the mushroom clouds of blood that form in the stream that runs at his feet, is classically Catholic in the literal-mindedness of the image. So too is the transubstantiation at the Last Supper, as Peter touches his lips with his fingers and realizes that the wine he just drank really has become blood. The film version of *Temptation* is rife with such images: Jesus dancing at the wedding at Cana; his stigmata during a confrontation at the Temple in Jerusalem; the powerful sense of pageantry that characterizes Scorsese's archetypal representation of Jesus's agony at Gethsemane ("it came right out of my childhood," Scorsese said). Perhaps the most striking manifestation of this self-conscious pageantry occurs in the final frames of the movie, which follows Jesus' death: the film is literally exposed *as* a film, revealing a riot of colors accompanied by a triumphant soundtrack: He has risen.[11]

Scorsese didn't only "Catholicize" *Temptation*; he also "Americanized" it. As was true of its sectarian dimension, this was not necessarily immediately apparent, especially given the amount of care given to making sure the film had a strong sense of historical verisimilitude in terms of its settings and costumes. The most obvious indications were the accents of the actors, who spoke in vernacular English. Though the movie was criticized, even mocked for this approach ("When a lion appears in the desert and asks, in the voice of Mr. Keitel, "Don't you rekonnize [sic] me?" the film is in danger of becoming silly," Janet Maslin wrote in an otherwise respectful review in the *New York Times*), it represented a conscious choice on Scorsese's part. Kazantzakis himself had written the book using informal Greek—his translator, P. A. Bien, speaks of "the essential Greekness of the novel, which, although set in the Holy Land, is peopled by Greeks in disguise"—and Scorsese made the film in a similar spirit:

> I was thinking about New York, Manhattan, 8th Avenue and 48th Street, the block where we shot *Taxi Driver* at night, a very dangerous area [at least through the 1980s, anyway] where there are drug pushers and pimps and prostitutes— it's my vision of hell. If you were to go there, those ten blocks from 42nd to 52nd Street on Eighth Avenue, and say, 'Blessed are the meek for they shall inherit the earth,' you'd get robbed, or beaten up, or killed. But if you go there and grab people and say, 'Look, I want to tell you about Jesus; I want to tell you about something he just said,' then it's a confrontation. I tried to do that with the Sermon on the Mount; we had to destroy the beautiful poetry of it, and convert it to suggest, almost, that he [Jesus] is getting the idea for the first time."

Scorsese and his collaborators capture this idea in a more humorous vein in a scene where Jesus informs Judas that the Messiah must die to fulfill the Scriptures, and Judas reacts with irritable confusion: "Every day you have a different plan! First it's love, then it's the ax, and now you have to die. What good could that do?" ("I can't help it," Jesus responds. "God only talks to me a little at a time.") It's important to note that these voices are not only those of Little Italy. Andre Gregory's John the Baptist, for example, has a Southern accent, and his preaching style is highly reminiscent of an evangelical Protestant preacher. And the Romans have English accents. ("Anyone in authority should have a British accent," Scorsese said at the time of what he called the "reverse snobbism" of his countrymen. "It just sounds authoritative to American ears.")

Other changes from the novel reflected a desire to respect contemporary political sensibilities. In the novel, the guardian angel who accompanies Jesus in his dream life is "a faithful little negro" boy who is always with him. Whatever its connotations in mid-century Greece, using such a figure in a late twentieth-century context would be grotesque for American audiences, recalling traditions of racist paternalism and conflating black skin with evil (the boy, after all, is Satan). In the movie, the angel is played by Juliette Caton, a cherubic girl with an English accent.

Scorsese also gave women a particular prominence in the movie. This is not solely an American preoccupation; in the Gospel of John, for example, it is Mary Magdalene who first sees the resurrected Jesus. And Kazantzakis gives her a particular prominence in the novel as well. But he was also prone to attribute ideas to women that would be grating to contemporary American ears, like Magdalene telling Jesus she and other women have little interest in hearing about an afterlife because "for us one moment with the man we love is everlasting paradise, one moment far from the man we love is everlasting hell. It is here on earth that we women live out our eternity." Women don't say such things in the movie; in fact Madgalene and Jesus' mother Mary are present in scenes—like the Last Supper— where they're typically represented as absent ("I just couldn't see him [Jesus] telling the women at the Last Supper, 'Wait in the kitchen,'" Scorsese explained, perhaps forgetting that in a traditional patriarchal society, he never would have had to). This is not to say he discarded Kazantzakis's view altogether. Indeed, despite some misgivings, he retained Jesus' inability to marry Magdalene as the the explanation for her prostitution. The movie also retains a relatively harsh treatment of the Virgin Mary, who is uncomprehending about and disappointed in her son; he, in turn, treats her dismissively (one thinks here of the Gospel of Mark, in which Jesus is told that his family is nearby and responds "Who are my mother and [my] brothers?" before going on to assert that anyone who does the will of God is his family). In the movie, though, Mary, played by Verna Bloom, has an air of dignity that she seems to lack in the novel.

Harvey Keitel used his role as Judas to strike a blow against intolerance, something that is of course timeless, but was also clearly on his mind as a contemporary concern. "Central to my desire to play Judas was my loathing, my abhorrence of prejudice," he said. "The notion that some man, woman or child's quality will be judged by the contours of their bones disgusts me and fills me with anger. That's why I had myself made up in the image of the stereotypical Jew." Verna Bloom was similarly inclined to draw more immediate parallels. "Marty told me that Mary was a mother, a Jewish mother. I'm a mother and I'm Jewish. As I worked on the part, I thought of my own son, Sam, and how much I loved him and would want to protect him. In fact, during the crucifixion scene, the identification I made became almost too painful to think about."

In the end, it was present–day issues and concerns—though not these present-day issues and concerns—that finally shaped the reception of *The Last Temptation of Christ* when it was released in 1988. A new wave of protests began before the film was even released, and a born-again Christian publicist hired by the studio resigned when Universal did not screen an early cut of the film for fundamentalists as promised (executives said the film was simply behind schedule, and could not meet the deadline). In July one evangelist offered to reimburse the cost of the film if the studio would hand it over to be destroyed. Two days later, nearly 200 members of the Fundamentalist Baptist Tabernacle of Los Angeles picketed the studio. In Britain Cardinal Basil Hume announced that the Catholic community should not see the film, because aspects of it would shock and outrage believers.

In the face of such opposition, Universal decided the best approach would be to preempt the building furor by releasing the film ahead of schedule, on August 12 instead of September 23. The late-summer premiere did steal a march on the opposition, though at the cost of the kind of attention a major studio feature typically gets in the fall. Nor did this altogether stop the protests in Los Angeles, San Francisco, Washington, Chicago, Seattle, and Toronto. Reaction was even stronger abroad: the film opened in Paris in late September to violent demonstrations and was banned in Israel and Greece. Intended by Scorsese as a work of art "made with deep religious feeling," to quote a public statement he released at the height of the controversy, *Temptation* was widely greeted as a prurient act of blasphemy.

Many critics and audiences—among them clergymen such as Paul Moore, the Episcopal bishop of New York—admired *Temptation*. Moreover, because it was made on a very modest budget, the film quickly earned back its production costs (one of the more amusing anecdotes Scorsese tells about making the movie involves creating an illusion of a large garrison of Romans by shooting the same five actors over and over again from different angles). To this day, *Temptation* is easily available on video, even if many stores decline to stock it. And Scorsese received an Academy Award nomination for Best Director.

For all that, in the broader context of Scorsese's career the movie nevertheless has the feel of a disappointment. Certainly Scorsese himself felt this way. "With *Last Temptation*, I wasn't totally satisfied," he said a decade after the film's release. "We never quite finished the picture because we had to release it so fast—though that's no excuse." Perhaps part of the problem was the way it juggled so many historical and contemporary elements, from the dialogue to the soundtrack. The combined effect of this, as Janet Maslin and other suggested, gave the film a somewhat wobbly quality. Perhaps, too, in its emphasis on struggle, *Temptation* betrays what Scorsese's friend Father Principe, in a widely cited quote, describes as a problem with the director's work: "too much Good Friday, and not enough Easter

Sunday" (indeed, the movie has literally nothing to say about the Resurrection). And despite the mindlessness on the part of some critics, there are clearly theological and psychological objections that one can take seriously. Still, all things considered, I myself believe the film was given far too much attention in some ways and far too little in others, and one objective in writing this chapter is to encourage more people to see it.

While *Temptation* has never achieved anything like the success of *The Great Gatsby* or *Gone with the Wind*, it nevertheless has a tremendous force and resonance in American life, particularly in regard to the American Dream. This is true in a way that has nothing to do with the directorial choices that Scorsese made in adapting the novel. Rather, it concerns the very thing that gave so many people such trouble: the premise that Jesus could have had a different, "better" life. To explain why, it might be useful to turn our attention back to the movie I've cast as the foil for *Temptation: It's a Wonderful Life*.

*　*　*

People would ask Willem [Dafoe], "How can you play Christ?" And he'd say, "I'm not really playing Christ. I'm just trying to play myself in that situation."

—*Leo Burmester, the apostle Nathaniel in*
The Last Temptation of Christ

I consider it one of the more painful scenes I have ever seen in a movie. George Bailey has just learned that his brother Harry, who was supposed to take over the family's savings and loan business after finishing college, has just gotten married—and received an exciting job offer from his new father-in-law in Buffalo. George gracefully allows his brother to leave town again and take the position, forcing him to surrender his own dream of college, just as he was forced to give up an extended world tour when his father died unexpectedly and he took over the family savings and loan business. But for the moment, he is indulging his disappointment alone on the

Bailey family front porch as the party celebrating Harry's nuptials goes on inside. Perhaps recognizing what he's thinking, George's mother suggests he visit Mary Hatch, a local girl who herself has just graduated. George pointedly walks in the opposite direction. Still, later that evening, he nevertheless finds himself at the Hatch home—just as his prescient mother phoned Mary to predict he would be. Learning that his visit was not a surprise, and irritated by the obvious manipulation on the part of these women, George behaves in a way that is the epitome of passive aggression, insisting that he doesn't want to be there even as he sits down, and frustrating every attempt Mary makes to engage him conversationally. The two get into a fight, and George leaves abruptly just as the phone rings: it's Sam Wainwright, George's old friend and Mary's current boyfriend (though Capra cuts to a shot of Wainwright attended to by women in his office, a clear signal of his waywardness). When George returns for his hat, Mary mentions he's there and Sam asks to speak to both them of them together. George and Mary share an uncomfortable intimacy as they listen together while Sam offers George a chance to get in on the ground floor of a plastics business he's starting (naturally, it was originally George's idea). But neither George nor Mary can pay much attention to Sam, because the electricity between them is finally so powerful that Mary drops the phone.

Far from embracing this intimacy, however, George resists it with all his might—this is not *his* dream. In anguished rage, he lashes out at Mary: "Now you listen to me," he tells her. "I don't want any plastics and I don't want any ground floors and I don't want to get married ever to anyone, you understand? I want to do what I want to do!" But in the end, George can't sustain this hostility in the face of Mary's tears. Their kisses, an amalgam of relief, sorrow, and love, are as difficult to watch as they are riveting. Capra releases the tension with an abrupt comic cut to the Bailey–Hatch wedding.

"I want to do what *I* want to do": is this not, from the self-inflicted travails of the Puritans to the self-gratifying videos of Madonna, a pithy encapsulation of the American Dream? In the end, George does not in fact do what he wants to do (though one can imagine far less happy outcomes than marrying Donna Reed). He instead surrenders what appears to be his destiny: helping other people attain their American Dreams by financing homes they can call their own. It's important to note, however, that this surrender, however, is finally a choice—no one *forces* George to stay in Bedford Falls. That's precisely what's so compelling, and so painful, about his presence there.

In *The Last Temptation of Christ*, Jesus also chooses to surrender to his destiny, and the drama of this particular rendition of his life stems from a vividly explored alternative. This cherished emphasis on choice, so central to American identity for slaves no less than religious dissidents (or, for that matter, affluent consumers), gives the story a special relevance for Americans, and in this regard it seems more than coincidental that the dream sequence in the novel (a little over fifty pages, or ten percent, of a five-hundred-page book) takes up twice as much space in the movie (a little over thirty minutes, or twenty percent, of a 160-minute film).[12] Whether or not we finally accept this particular version of Christ's passion, some notion of choice is absolutely indispensable to the American imagination. Notwithstanding the pronouncements of athletic coaches building sports dynasties, the concept of destiny is a deeply problematic one for a people who not only believe they have the freedom to make choices about what they're going to do with their lives, but really seem to believe that they can achieve the happiness they have a national birthright to pursue.

This, finally, is what's so scary about *It's a Wonderful Life* and, especially, *The Last Temptation of Christ*. Both movies depict people who choose to give up their freedom in the name of some larger purpose. In so doing, they paradoxically create an uncomfortably viable option of denial—not as a tale of misplaced altruism or as a cautionary tale of over-involvement, but as a credible alternative to the American Dream as it is commonly represented. This creates a sense of guilt, even pressure, until you remember you don't *have* to give up some of the things Jesus only dreamt about: after all, *you're* not God. Still, there's always the prospect that, like Willem Dafoe, you could end up in a similar situation. And who knows: you might even give a good performance.

But a satisfactory resolution of one's spiritual imperatives may not necessarily demand that one abandon the American Dream entirely. The Puritans, after all, did what they wanted to do: love God as they saw fit (however imperfectly). That was a long time ago. Still, there are other, living American Dreams that may be even more worthy. And so I will end by returning to the beginning, with a Dream of Freedom embodied by an American King.

UPLIFTING FIGURE

Martin Luther King, Jr. at a press conference, November 1964. No one has done more to redeem the moral integrity of the American Dream by giving it an unequivocally Christian dimension. As such, King remains a shining example to Catholics of the transformative possibilities of the double consciousness so vividly described by W. E. B. DuBois. *(Photo by Dick DeMarsico from the World-Telegram & Sun Collection of the Library of Congress)*

Conclusion

THE SOULS OF KINGS

"**I** should like to discuss with you some aspects of the American Dream," the Reverend Martin Luther King, Jr., told the graduating students of Lincoln University, a historically black institution in Chester County, Pennsylvania, in June 1961. "For in a sense, America is essentially a dream, a dream as yet unfulfilled."

Few figures in American history expressed the promises and perplexity of the American Dream better than King. In the eighteenth century, its premiere apostle was Thomas Jefferson, who codified it in the Declaration of Independence—and struggled with its implications for the rest of his (slaveholding) life. In the nineteenth century, it was Abraham Lincoln, who gave the Dream a new lease on life in fusing union and freedom in the Gettysburg Address (the school where King spoke, chartered as Ashmun Institute in 1854, was renamed for Lincoln in 1866). And in the twentieth century it was King who, in an unforgettable speech at the Lincoln Memorial now familiar to schoolchildren from one end of the nation to the other, told his fellow Americans of his own dream: that his children "will one day live in a nation where they will not be judged by the color of their skin but by the content of their character."

There are a number of important aspects to King's Dream that are worth noting here. The first is its essentially religious character. Amid the political and social tumult of the 1950s and 1960s, it is easy to forget that the Civil Rights Movement began in Christian churches, and that much of the subsequent activism propelling the movement, whether in car pools, fund drives, or voter registration, was rooted in church membership and organization. King himself was first and foremost a (Baptist) clergyman, and his quest rested on bedrock moral values of love that nothing—not the plagiarism of his doctoral dissertation at Boston University, sexual infidelity over the course of his marriage, or the multiple failures he and others endured throughout his career in the movement—could compromise. He was, like all of us, a sinner. And in the scope of his ambitions and the price he paid for them, he comes about as close as any man in the United States ever has to being a saint.

Second, King dreamed with a profound awareness of American history. Indeed, one of the most striking things about King's American Dream is that it was so utterly American, less a matter of demanding something new than a quest to honor widely shared ideals. Like Lincoln, he often referred to the Founding Fathers, and situated the work of the Civil Rights Movement to the origins of the nation. The students participating in the antisegregation lunch counter sit-ins of the early sixties, he stated repeatedly, "are taking our whole nation back to those great wells of democracy which were dug deep by the Founding Fathers in the formulation of the Constitution and the Declaration of Independence. In sitting down at the lunch counters, they are in reality standing up for the best of the American Dream." King expressed a variation on this idea in his famous "I Have a Dream" speech when he described it as "a dream deeply rooted in the American Dream that one day this nation will rise up and live out the true meaning of its creed—we hold these truths to be self-evident, that all men are created equal." The power of King's appeal lay precisely in the way he asked his fellow Americans to live by the values they so ardently professed.

Still, despite this appeal to common values, a third major aspect of King's dream is that it aroused so much opposition. Nowadays, virtually no one—not even those conservatives who either would have (or actually did) condemn King as a troublemaker—would deny the validity of many of his major objectives, and much of the opposition to policies like affirmative action (which King supported) are cast as antithetical to his core values of "freedom" and "opportunity." To be meaningful in any concrete sense, however, such words must be more than abstractions. Instruments of the Dream such as education, health care, and other forms of public good should be widely and easily accessible to everyone, not merely theoretical possibilities for those who have the income, family connections, or mere luck to procure them. Freedom was defined in terms of equality.

Finally, and most importantly, King's dream was never simply an aspiration for its own—or *his* own—sake. It was inextricably woven with his religious faith, animated by a belief in improvement in this world as preparation for the next. One of the paradoxes of King's life was that this black man, who was inevitably a second-class citizen in some respects, was a prince in others: the son of the pastor of the largest black congregation in America, educated in the best schools (black *and* white, North *and* South), and a jet-setter in some ways more at ease with European royalty than ordinary black folk. Yet, after some initial uncertainty about his vocation, he showed extraordinary sensitivity to the suffering of these people and made it his own. He was, in a very important sense, an American Moses, as he seemed to recognize on the final night of his life. "Like anybody, I would like to live a long life," he said in Memphis, a city he was visiting to support striking black sanitation workers. "Longevity has its place. But I'm not concerned about that now. I just want to do God's will. And He's allowed me to go up to the mountain. And I've looked over. And I've seen the promised land."

To put the matter a little differently, King had an unusually well-developed sense of double consciousness: of white and black, privilege and deprivation, success and failure, dream and reality. He had both a clear set of goals (social justice) as well as a clear sense of limits (nonviolence). He loved his country, but that very love for it made him critical of it and interested in alternative visions, like that of Mohandas Gandhi in particular and the experiences peoples of the Third World in general, that could inform his own. He cared deeply about what happened on earth, but that care was tempered by an awareness of an afterlife.[13]

In these and in other ways, King remains a role model for American Catholics. He simultaneously is, and is not, one of us. Throughout this book, I have made implicit as well as explicit comparisons between Catholic and Protestant worldviews. In particular, I've tried to show how the Protestant imagination of the Puritans, which began from Calvinist premises, paradoxically gave way to a preparationist ethos that placed special emphasis on individual improvement, an emphasis that has become the hallmark of an American Dream embraced by Catholics, Jews, agnostics, and atheists no less than Protestants. This ethos, as attractive as it can seem, carries with it less attractive aspects, too, among them a stress on personal responsibility that can lead to denials of collective obligation and commitments to reform that can be arrogant, both in terms of personal pride for things that are not solely one's own doing and in assuming others must think and act the same way. King's life and death, however, vividly demonstrate that such excesses are not inevitable. They also display the most attractive aspects of Protestantism, among them the pursuit and realization of goals that are entirely appropriate from sacred as well as secular standpoints.

But the realization of any goal, religious or otherwise, cannot finally be the measure of the American Dream's validity: it simply happens too rarely, and is too ambiguous, even insufficient, to be truly satisfying when it does. Nor, I suspect, can we finally content ourselves with the familiar assertion that it's the journey, not the destination that matters. It's true as far as it goes, but in the end, a journey can't really *be* a journey without *some* sense of an end. And if life is not a journey, then it can be little more than a series of all too fleeting sensations.

Instead, I'd like to leave you with the observations of the late Christopher Lasch, a self-described child of "militant secularists" who died in 1994 after a highly iconoclastic career in which he consistently engaged and criticized the leftist tradition from which he sprang. In his 1991 book *The True and Only Heaven*, Lasch makes an interesting distinction between hope and optimism. Optimism, in his definition, is confidence in Progress, a belief in imminent improvement rooted in the American historical experience of economic growth and the sunny promises of the American Dream. Optimism rests on expectation, and can curdle quickly into disillusionment if expectations are not regularly met.

Hope, by contrast, is subtly but significantly different:

> Hope implies a deep-seated trust in life that appears absurd to those who lack it. It rests on confidence not so much in the future as in the past. It derives from early memories—no doubt distorted, overlaid with later memories, and thus not wholly reliable as a guide to any factual reconstruction of

past events—in which the experience of order and content-
ment was so intense that subsequent disillusionments cannot
dislodge it. Such experience leaves as its residue the unshak-
able conviction, not that the past was better than the present
[which Lasch specifically repudiates as disabling nostalgia],
but that trust is never completely displaced, even though it is
never completely justified either and therefore destined
inevitably to disappointments.

These words describe my sense of American Catholicism. The
past here is not only that of American history, which I claim as my
own, but also my personal experience of my religion and the knowl-
edge that it extends far beyond that of American history, reaching
back to a time long before the division of Catholic and Protestant—
and, for that matter, the division of Christian and Jew. It is a past
that can be experienced on any given Sunday, and one that lives on
as a memory that can shape a future where little seems certain
except the eventual death of the American Dream.

For the Dream, like all living things, will die someday. The task
before us is less a quest for immortality than an obligation to
improve the quality of its life for ourselves and our children. We
celebrate, if not actually honor, the idea of a country where all men
and women are created equal. But if American Dreams are to have
any validity—and, in the end, if they are to have any *vitality*—they
will only be so to the extent that they are rooted in the lives, deaths,
and, yes, the rebirths of Kings.

ENDNOTES

1. The term "Congregational" has two distinct but overlapping meanings, which can be confusing for students of church history. One definition of congregationalism, lower-case "c," to be discussed in a little more depth below, describes a form of church organization. In this usage, any number of Protestant churches may be congregational. The other definition, upper-case "C," refers to the specific Christian sect of the Puritans both before and after their merger with the Separatists of Plymouth.

2. At the same time, the Puritans had strong impulses to maintain and extend what they had gained, even when doing so was in direct violation of their original doctrines. This problem was on vivid display in the debate over the so–called Halfway Covenant of 1662, an issue which, perhaps unlike some other controversies, really touched Puritans where they lived. This dispute involved how to handle the church membership of children. The founders had been clear, even emphatic, about who could join a congregation: only those who had rendered convincing testimony of their conversion. Almost by definition, children were incapable of doing so. Case closed, said some Puritans. Others, however, pulled by ties that seem to transcend time and place, could not bear the thought of denying their children what they themselves most cherished. Under the pressure of such sentiment, Congregationalists developed a doctrine whereby children could be provisionally accepted ("halfway") into the church, pending a later confirmation-type of experience. (We see here the roots of the common Protestant experience of being "born again.") Such was but one example of how the Puritans were pulled, seemingly inexorably, away from the purity of their original theological commitments.

3. Not all American politicians succumbed to the insidious appeal of anti–immigrant and anti–Catholic bias. "I am not a Know–Nothing," Abraham Lincoln wrote to an old friend who queried his political orientation in 1855. "That fact is certain. How could I be? How can anyone who abhors the oppression of negroes, be in favor of degrading a class of white people?" To Lincoln, discrimination against immigrants was part of a larger pattern. "Our progress in degeneracy appears to me to be pretty rapid," he continued. "As a nation we began by declaring that *all men are created equal.* We now practically read it, 'all men are created equal, *except Negroes.*' When the Know-Nothings get in control, it will read 'all men are created equal, except negroes, *and foreigners, and catholics.*' When it comes to this I should prefer emigrating to some country where they make no pretence of loving liberty—to Russia, for instance, where despotism can be taken pure, without the base alloy of hypocrisy." See *Lincoln: Speeches and Writings 1832–1858,* edited by Don Fehrenbacher (New York: Library of America, 1989), 363.

4. One of the inside jokes in the novel is that "Gatsby's" name is a play on "gat," a slang term for gun, derived from the Gatling gun, a British machine gun used during the First World War.

5. One of the bizarre ironies of *The Great Gatsby* is that Meyer Wolfsheim, who is almost certainly Jewish, apparently runs "The Swastika Holding Company" (178). As Matthew Bruccoli explains in the explanatory notes included in the authorized text, swastikas did not have the widespread anti–Semitic connotations in the 1920s they would have once Adolf Hitler came to power in Germany in 1933.

6. Actually, James is an Anglicized version of Jacob, which of course *is* a standard Jewish name, but Jews have generally steered clear of James in the Christian era. Thanks to my friends Jaime Silverman and Ron Afzal for help on this point.

7. There's one small but significant difference: Rhett describes Melanie as a *very* great lady, which seems justified given all she endures. In this context, it's interesting that Melly is not Catholic, which not only (sensibly) suggests that virtue knows no sectarian boundaries, but also, given Ellen's death during the war, Melly's survival of it, and Scarlett's evolving attitudes, also implies that Catholicism is somehow not quite relevant to the modern, post–Civil War world. (For the "great" descriptions of the women, see *GWTW*, 60, 1025.)

8. Later, Scarlett commits similar grammatical slippage. "I wonder what our grandchildren will be like!" she says to Rhett while still married to Frank Kennedy, presumably thinking about the next generation generally. "Are you suggesting by 'our' that you and I will have mutual grandchildren?" Rhett replies jokingly. "Fie, Mrs. Kennedy!" (See *GWTW*, 203, 681.)

9. By coincidence, the designer of this book also happens to be named Madonna: Madonna Gauding.

10. There are, in fact, manifold differences between the novel and movie, some of which I will describe below as they relate to the religious and national reorientation of the film. For the most part, however, I am going to eschew an extended discussion of these differences (e.g., the absence of Barabbas from the movie, or Scorsese's use of a flame rather than an archangel as the third temptation in the desert) in the interest of keeping this chapter relatively concise and focused on the themes of this book.

11. In a television broadcast of *Temptation* on the Bravo network in the spring of 2000, a voiceover at the end of the film reported that this shot was actually an accident, the result of a camera running out of film while filming Willem Dafoe on the cross. One would like to think there was an element of divine intervention here.

12. "I thought it was too long," Kazantzakis's widow, Eleni, said of the dream sequence in the movie. "But Nikos did the same thing. I told him while I was typing the manuscript that the temptation scene was too long." See Kelly, 239.

13. So did Abraham Lincoln. I hope the reader will forebear to hear one

more quote, this one written as unpublished fragment when Lincoln was running for Senate 1858. He lost the race, but the following passage showcases the moral clarity that girded his conception of the American Dream, one that decisively shaped his behavior as president:

> I have never professed an indifference to the honors of official station; and were I to do so now, I should only make myself ridiculous. Yet I have never failed—do not now fail—to remember that in the republican cause there is a higher aim than that of mere office. I have not allowed myself to forget that the abolition of the Slave-trade by Great Britain was agitated a hundred years before it was a final success; that the measure had its open fire-eating opponents; its stealthy "don't care" opponents; its inferior race opponents; its [anti] negro equality opponents; and its religion and good order opponents; that all these opponents got offices, and their adversaries got none. But I have also remembered that though they blazed, like tallow-candles for a century, at last they flickered in the socket, died out, stank in the dark for a brief season and were remembered no more, even by the smell . . . Remembering these things I cannot regard it as possible that the higher object of this contest may not be completely attained within the term of my natural life.

See Abraham Lincoln, "Fragment on the Struggle Against Slavery," in *Speeches and Writings 1832–1858*, edited by Don Fehrenbacher (New York: The Modern Library), 437–438.

SOURCES AND NOTES

INTRODUCTION: THE SOULS OF CATHOLIC FOLK

xv. *"It is a peculiar sensation"*: W. E. B. DuBois, *The Souls of Black Folk* (1903; New York: Penguin, 1989), 5.

xvi. *relatively small degree of integration*: For more on the black Catholic experience, see Cyprian Davis, O.S.B., *The History of Black Catholics in the United States* (New York: Crossroad, 1990).

xviii. *Bruce Springsteen's music*: Jim Cullen, *Born in the U.S.A.: Bruce Springsteen and the American Tradition* (New York: HarperCollins, 1997). See chapter 7, "Inherited Imagination," on Springsteen's Catholic heritage.

xx. *Andrew Greeley has been contributing for many years*: Greeley has written and talked about popular culture in a variety of media regularly over the last fifteen years. For an elucidation of his underlying intellectual framework, see his chapter "Do Catholics Imagine Differently?" in *The Catholic Myth: The Behavior and Beliefs of American Catholics* (New York: Collier, 1990), 34–64. His example, and especially that of Paul Giles, who takes a much more rigorous scholarly approach in *Catholic Arts and Fictions: Culture, Ideology, Aesthetics* (New York: Cambridge University Press, 1992), were influential in shaping my own perspective on the role of religion in popular culture and vice versa.

xxi. *no history book ever has, or likely ever will:* For more on this point, see *Jim Cullen, The Civil War in Popular Culture: A Reusable Past* (Washington, D.C.: Smithsonian Institution Press, 1995), chapter 3 (65–107).

xxiii. *ordinary people from the ground up:* Jay Dolan, *The American Catholic Experience: A History from Colonial Times to the Present* (1931; Garden City, NY: Doubleday, 1985).

CHAPTER ONE: THE COMPLEXITIES OF THE AMERICAN DREAM

4. *"the charm of anticipated success":* Alexis de Tocqueville, *Democracy in America*, volume 2, translated by Phillips Bradley (1840; New York: Vintage Books, 1990), 71.

4. *"that dream of a land":* James Truslow Adams, *The Epic of America* (Garden City, NY: Blue Ribbon Books, 1941), 404

4. *pay three dollars:* Allan Nevins, *James Truslow Adams: Historian of the American Dream* (Urbana, IL: University of Illinois Press, 1968), 68 (footnote).

7. *"As I read":* Mary Antin, *The Promised Land* (1912; New York: Penguin, 1997), 177 (italics in original).

9. *two-thirds of American households:* "To Surprise of Many Experts, Housing Boom Keeps Rolling," the *New York Times,* May 27, 1999, A1. The actual figure cited by the *Times* was 66.7%.

9. *Abraham Levitt:* Information on the Levitt family and the communities they designed comes from a variety of sources, the most important of which is Kenneth Jackson's *Crabgrass Frontier: The Suburbanization of the United States* (New York: Oxford University Press, 1985).

11. *not a single resident:* Jackson, 241.

12. *fast, easy prosperity:* On the role of gambling in colonial America and in other periods, see John M. Findlay, *People of Chance: Gambling in American Society from Jamestown to Las Vegas* (New York: Oxford University Press, 1986).

12. *"When I was a boy":* Presley quoted in Greil Marcus, *Mystery Train: Images of America in Rock & Roll Music,* third revised edition (1972; New York: Plume, 1990, 134). For a very similar quote, made when Presley received an award from the Jaycees as one of the nation's Ten Most Outstanding Men of the Year for 1970, see Peter Guralnick's biography of Presley, *Careless Love: The Unmaking of Elvis Presley* (Boston: Little, Brown, 1999), 429.

CHAPTER TWO: THE ANTI-CATHOLIC ORIGINS OF THE AMERICAN DREAM

17. *"This Afternoon's Entertainment"*: John Adams to Abigail Adams in *The Adams Family Chronicles*, Series II, *The Adams Family Correspondence*, volume 1 (Cambridge, MA: Harvard University Press, 1963), 167.

18. *"Comrades"*: Cortés quoted in Jay Dolan, *The American Catholic Experience: A History from Colonial Times to the Present* (Garden City, NY: Doubleday, 1985), 17.

19. *the case of the Cimarrons*: Background on the Cimarron-English alliance and early English colonization planning comes from Edmund Morgan, *American Slavery, American Freedom: The Ordeal of Colonial Virginia* (1975; New York: Norton, 1995), 10–18.

21. *"We call you Puritans"*: Alan Heimert and Andrew Delbanco, *The American Puritans: A Narrative Anthology* (Cambridge, MA: Harvard University Press, 1985), 1.

22. *"began both deeply to apprehend"*: excerpts from Bradford included in Heimert and Delbanco, 53.

23. *"God Almighty:"* Winthrop's sermon is included in Heimert and Delbanco, 81–92.

26. *"These are the days"*: Anne Bradstreet, "A Dialogue Between Old England and New; Concerning Their Present Troubles, Anno 1642," in *Early American Poetry*, edited by Jane Donahue Eberwein (Madison, Wis.: University of Wisconsin Press, 1978), 29.

29. *as one Puritan scholar*: Andrew Delbanco, *The Puritan Ordeal* (Cambridge, MA: Harvard University Press, 1989), 51.

31. *feared* losing *than gaining*: The backward–looking dimension of the American Revolution is emphasized in much recent scholarship on the subject. The foundation for much of this scholarship is Bernard Bailyn's magisterial *Ideological Origins of the American Revolution* (Cambridge, MA: Harvard University Press, 1967). See especially chapter 5, "Transformation," 160–229.

34. *sole surviving transcript*: For excerpts, see Heimert and Delbanco, 154–163.

35. *"So convenient a thing"*: Benjamin Franklin, *Autobiography* (1790; New York: Oxford University Press, 1996), 36 (emphasis in original).

40. *"I think that the Catholic religion"*: Alexis de Tocqueville, *Democracy in America*, volume 1. Translated by Phillips Bradley (1835; New York: Vintage, 1990), 300–301.

40. *"The men of our days"*: Alexis de Tocqueville, *Democracy in America*, volume 2. Translated by Phillips Bradley (1840; New York: Vintage, 1990), 29.

40. *One True Church*: Tocqueville, volume 2, 30.

CHAPTER THREE: FATAL ATTRACTION: THE CASE OF JAY GATSBY

45. *"I am ashamed to say"*: *The Letters of F. Scott Fitzgerald*, edited by Andrew Turnbull (1963; New York: Scribner/Macmillan, 1990), 325.

46. *decades to come*: Charles Morris, *American Catholic: The Saints and Sinners Who Built America's Most Powerful Church* (New York: Vintage, 1998), 109, 113.

46. *Fitzgerald's family*: Information on Fitzgerald's early ancestry can be found in "The Colonial Ancestors of Francis Scott Key Fitzgerald," an essay by his daughter, Scottie Fitzgerald Smith, included in Matthew Bruccoli's *Some Epic Sort of Grandeur: The Life of F. Scott Fitzgerald* (New York: Harcourt Brace Jovanovich, 1981), a biography by the premiere contemporary Fitzgerald scholar. Other important sources on Fitzgerald's background and life include Andrew Turnbull, *F. Scott Fitzgerald: A Biography* (1962; New York: Collier, 1988), Arthur Mizener, *The Far Side of Paradise: A Biography of F. Scott Fitzgerald* (Cambridge, MA: Riverside Press, 1949), and Joan M. Allen, *Candles and Carnival Lights: The Catholic Sensibility of F. Scott Fitzgerald* (New York: New York University Press, 1978).

48. *"a dazzling, golden thing"*: Fitzgerald quoted in Turnbull, 78.

48. *"last year as a Catholic"*: Fitzgerald quoted in Bruccoli, 52, 89, and Paul Giles, *American Catholic Arts and Fictions: Culture, Ideology, Aesthetics* (New York: Cambridge University Press, 1992), 170.

49. *allow burial*: The circumstances surrounding Fitzgerald's funeral, while clear on the basic facts, differ slightly in some of his biographies (such as the specific basis of his exclusion from a Catholic burial). Joan Allen makes an effort to sort out the discrepancies and offers a relatively detailed account in *Candles and Carnival Lights*, 141–145.

49. *George Washington and Ignatius Loyola*: Allen, 9.

49. *"His books have no religious insights"*: Leslie Fiedler, "Some Notes on F. Scott Fitzgerald," in *An End to Innocence: Essays on Culture and Politics* (Boston: Beacon Press, 1955), 181; F. Scott Fitzgerald, *Tender Is the Night* (New York: Scribners, 1934), 312.

50. *"Despite the generalization"*: Bruccoli, 95–96.

50. *underestimate the degree*: A number of recent scholars of American Catholic culture have noted this tendency. For examples of such religious myopia with specific reference to Fitzgerald, see Giles (who makes the point with a number of other figures as well) and Allen.

50. *"I am half black Irish"*: Fitzgerald quoted in Bruccoli, 25.

51. *20,000 copies*: Claudia Roth Pierpont makes the claim the novel sells more in a month than it did in Fitzgerald's lifetime in her article "For Love and Money: An Early Version of Fitzgerald's Great American Novel Is Resurrected," the *New Yorker*, July 3, 2000. In the afterword of the 1992 edition of the novel, publisher Charles Scribner III says the first printing of *Gatsby* was 20,000

copies, and that a second printing of 3,000 never sold out before Fitzgerald's death (203). Using these figures, one can estimate the book was selling a quarter of a million copies annually at the start of this century.

52. *"a colossal accident":* F. Scott Fitzgerald, *The Great Gatsby,* the authorized text (1925; New York Scribner's 1992), 156.

55. *"was intended to be a picture":* Fitzgerald quoted in Bruccoli, 192.

55. *"being mean to an old lady":* F. Scott Fitzgerald, "Absolution," in *The Stories of F. Scott Fitzgerald,* edited by Malcolm Cowley (1951; New York: Scribner's, 1986), 162–163.

55. *"a wild, proud anger":* "Absolution," 166.

56. *"the sharp tap of cloven hoofs":* "Absolution," 169.

56. *"When a lot of people":* "Absolution," 171.

57. *"It amazed him.":* The Great Gatsby, 155–156.

58. *"blossomed like a flower":* The Great Gatsby,*117.

58. *inverted parody of Mass:* As Allen notes, "Gatsby celebrates the Sabbath with secular love feasts which glorify the sensual life" (103). For more on the specifically Catholic imagery that suffuses the novel, see *Candles and Carnival Lights,* 101–116.

58. *"there was something gorgeous":* The Great Gatsby, 6.

58. *"I guess I am":* Letters of F. Scott Fitzgerald, 63.

58. *"you can't repeat the past":* The Great Gatsby, 116.

59. *"You can fool me":* The Great Gatsby, 165–167.

59. *his father:* Allen is one of a number of people who points this out. See page 109 of *Candles and Carnival Lights.*

59. *"Through all he said":* The Great Gatsby, 118.

60. *"worth the whole damn bunch":* The Great Gatsby, 162.

60. *"Gatsby believed":* The Great Gatsby, 189.

61. *"cheap Irish love of defeat":* Hemingway quoted in Giles, 173.

CHAPTER FOUR: INCOMPLETE DENIAL: THE CASE OF SCARLETT O'HARA

65. *"[Scarlett O'Hara] obeyed":* Margaret Mitchell, *Gone with the Wind* (1936; New York: Macmillan, 1986), 335. Subsequent references will be denoted as *GWTW.*

66. *"Southerners have been wonderful":* Margaret Mitchell to Sidney Howard, November 21, 1936, in *Margaret Mitchell's* Gone with the Wind Letters, 1936–1939, edited by Richard Harwell (New York: Macmillan, 1976), 92–94.

66. *Mitchell felt no similar commitment:* Mitchell and her friend are quoted, and her religious renunciation is discussed, in Darden Asbury Pyron, *Southern Daughter: The Life of Margaret Mitchell* (New York: Oxford University Press, 1991), 92–93, 479.

68. *"The Klan!":* GWTW, 798.

68. *Her family's roots:* Mitchell's genealogical background is discussed extensively in Pyron, 9–27, the source of most of the information presented here. See also Finis Farr, *Margaret Mitchell of Atlanta* (New York: Morrow, 1965) and Anne Edwards, *Road to Tara: The Life of Margaret Mitchell* (New Haven: Ticknor & Fields, 1983).

69. *"all daring":* Stephens Mitchell quoted in Edwards, 66.

69. *May Belle was an active force:* On May Belle Mitchell's role in opposing Watson, see Pyron, 39.

70. *Atlanta race riot:* Pyron describes Mitchell's recollections. See pages 31–32.

70. *"One of the earliest purposes":* Margaret Mitchell to Ruth Tallman, July 30, 1937, GWTW Letters.

72. *"[W]hen Mrs. Wilkes":* GWTW, 50.

72. *Years later, Gerald's funeral:* GWTW, 706–709.

72. *Indeed, unlike her mother:* The Mitchell womens' educations are discussed in Pyron, 25–26; 62–63.

74. *"therapy for my [injured] leg":* Edwards, 145.

74. *Mitchell chased down Latham:* Pyron's version of this story is the most detailed and analytical. See *Southern Daughter,* 295–301.

75. *myself among them:* See the chapter on GWTW in Jim Cullen, *The Civil War in Popular Culture: A Reusable Past* (Washington, D.C.: Smithsonian Institution Press, 1995).

75. *"When Scarlett was a child":* GWTW, 60.

75. *"Is the brat baptized":* GWTW, 64.

75. *"The kneeling figures":* GWTW, 70.

76. *"Scarlett wanted":* GWTW, 60.

76. *"Ellen would be shocked":* GWTW, 61.

76. *By this point in the story:* On the circumstances of the O'Hara marriage, see GWTW, 53–54. Apropos of my footnote regarding Rhett's description of Melanie and Ellen as great ladies, it may be worth noting here that Ellen's mother is *also* described as "a very great lady" by Gerald's brother, James. Scarlett notwithstanding, it appears that as far as Mitchell is concerned, some Southern daughters really *do* take after their mothers.

77. *". . . Even the banked flowers":* GWTW, 173.

78. *"I am heartbroken"*: GWTW, 199.

79. *"Dear God!"*: GWTW, 347.

79. *"Nothing her mother had taught her"*: GWTW, 434.

79. *"Occasionally, Scarlett wondered"*: GWTW, 507, 510.

80. *"The congregation of the Episcopal Church"*: GWTW, 906.

80. *she's considering an abortion*: GWTW, 882–883.

80. *"Oh, God"*: GWTW, 961.

80. *"God would punish her"*: GWTW, 829–830.

81. *"Confess your sins"*: GWTW, 946–947.

81. *"I'm sure"*: GWTW, 936. Rhett's allusion to "lusting in your heart" comes from Matthew 5:28: "But I say to you, everyone who looks at a woman with lust has already committed adultery with her in his heart."

82. *"She never even suspected"*: GWTW, 1015.

82. *"Ever since I've known you"*: GWTW, 1032.

83. *"Happy?"*: Sinatra quoted in J. Randy Taraborelli, *Sinatra: Behind the Legend* (New York: Birch Lane Press, 1997), 56.

83. *Sinatra's lifestyle*: For more on the singer and the American Dream, see Jim Cullen, "Fool's Paradise: Frank Sinatra and the American Dream," in *Popular Culture in American History*, edited by Jim Cullen (Oxford: Blackwell, 2000).

CHAPTER FIVE: LIKE A HERETIC: THE CASE OF MADONNA

85. *"I won't be happy"*: *Madonna: In Her Own Words*, edited by Mick St. Michael (London, Omnibus Press, 1999), 62.

85. *"our lady of constant makeovers"*: Edna Gunderson, "Face-to-Face with Madonna," *USA Today*, December 11, 1996. The piece is included in *The Madonna Companion: Two Decades of Commentary*, edited by Allan Metz and Carol Benson (New York: Schirmer, 1999), 74–79.

85. *"The freeing of the priest"*: The Wildmon piece, "This Video is Offensive to Believers," was part of a pro-and-con package paired with a pro–Madonna piece by publicist Liz Rosenberg, published in *USA Today* in 1989. See *The Madonna Companion*, 181–183.

85. *"Embodying Subaltern Memory"*: Cindy Patton, "Embodying Subaltern Memory: Kinesthesia and the Problematics of Gender and Race" in *The Madonna Connection: Representational Politics, Subcultural Identities, and Cultural Theory*, edited by Cathy Schwictenberg (Boulder, CO: Westview Press, 1993), 81–106; bell hooks, "Power to the Pussy: We Don't Want to Be Wannabe Dicks in Drag," in *Madonnarama: Essays on Sex and Popular Culture*, edited by Lisa Frank and Paul Smith (Pittsburgh: Cleis Press, 1993), 65–80.

85. *Intelligent analysis from many quarters:* See, for example, Joseph Sobran's piece "Sex and the Single Girl" from the *National Review,* August 12, 1991, and Daniel Harris's "Make My Rainy Day" from *The Nation,* June 8, 1992, both of which are included in *The Madonna Companion.* Both of these pieces are critical of Madonna, those who write about her, or both, but as future citations in the piece will show, I think there have been many positive and useful things said about her from a number of writers.

87. *"I sometimes think":* Madonna quoted in Norman King, *Madonna: The Book* (New York: Morrow, 1991), 241.

87. *"Growing up":* Denise Worrell, "Madonna," *Time,* May 27, 1985, included in *The Madonna Connection,* 40.

88. *Carole Lombard and Marilyn Monroe:* When, four years later, she was asked by a different magazine about her heroines or role models, she responded by saying, "It's weird, people always ask me that question and I can't think of anybody specifically. [long pause] I think a few nuns, I thought they were pretty incredible. They all seemed powerful and perfect. And really clean [laughs]. For a while I was obsessed with being a nun, for those reasons. Then, when I realized that nuns didn't have a sex life, I was incredibly disenchanted." See Becky Johnston, "Confession of a Catholic Girl," *Interview,* May 1989. Reprinted in *The Madonna Companion,* 67.

88. *"It wasn't until":* In Her Own Words, 68.

89. *working-class Italian Catholicism:* See, for example, Camille Paglia's comments in two pieces included in her essay collection *Sex, Art, and American Culture* (New York: Vintage, 1992). Andrew Greeley makes a similar line of argument, albeit from a more orthodox point of view, in "Like a Catholic: Madonna's Challenge to Her Church," *America,* May 13, 1989, 447–449. For a sustained exploration of vernacular Italian–American Catholic religious style, see Robert Orsi, *The Madonna of 115th Street: Faith and Community in Italian Harlem, 1880–1950* (New Haven: Yale University Press, 1985).

89. *"We used to get up":* Johnston, 64–65.

89. *"I also remember":* Johnston, 64.

90. *"I got into":* Johnston, 64.

90. *"I was afraid":* Johnston, 65.

90. *feigned surprise:* On her meeting with Lang, see Christopher Anderson, "Madonna Rising: The Wild and Funky Years in New York," *New York,* October 14, 1991, in *The Madonna Companion,* 87–89.

91. *Madonna was principally the lyricist:* "I don't write music, and I don't read music," Madonna explained to Johnston (70).

91. Billboard *top twenty:* See the periodically updated *Billboard Book of Top 40 Hits,* edited by Joel Whitburn (New York: Billboard Publications, 1985), 198.

92. *"Madonna's voice"*: Simon Frith, "The Sound of *Erotica*: Pain, Power, and Pop," in *Madonnarama*, 88.

93. *Madonna was a feminist*: This distinction drawn here between equality feminism and difference feminism is elucidated in "Feminism at the Crossroads," a talk given by poet and *Nation* columnist Katha Pollitt in 1993 and published in the Spring 1994 issue of *Dissent* magazine. I encountered the piece in *Left, Right, and Center: Voices from Across the Political Spectrum*, edited by Robert Atwan and Jon Roberts (Boston: Bedford/St. Martin's Press, 1996), 239–244.

94. *top ten*: *Billboard Book of Top 40 Hits*, 198.

95. *"When I went"*: Worrell, "Madonna!" 45.

95. *one iota*: This point is made by Luc Sante in an August 1990 piece on Madonna in the *New Republic*: "If, at this point, there is any aspect of Madonna's act that seems independent of calculation, it is her preoccupation with Catholic mysteries." See "Unlike a Virgin" in *The Madonna Companion*, 237.

96. *"Once you're a Catholic"*: Bill Zehme, "Madonna: The *Rolling Stone* Interview" *Rolling Stone*, March 23, 1989, 180.

96. *"Anyone who listens"*: Greeley, "Like a Catholic," 448. Elements of this piece were incorporated into *The Catholic Myth: The Behavior and Belief of American Catholics* (New York: Collier, 1990), 277–285.

97. *"extremely defeated"*: Madonna discusses her depression and Penn's encouragement in Johnston, 70, 72. See also *In Her Own Words*, 47.

99. *lapsed Catholic*: For more on Warhol's Catholicism, see Paul Giles, *American Catholic Arts and Fictions: Culture, Ideology, Aesthetics* (New York: Cambridge University Press, 1992), 278–284.

102. *"if slavery is not wrong"*: Abraham Lincoln to Albert G. Hodges in *Lincoln: Speeches and Writings*, edited by Don Fehrenbacher (New York: Library of America, 1989), volume 2, 585.

102. *"incorporated more"*: Johnston, 59. For Madonna's own description of the video, from which I have drawn my own summary of it, see Stephen Holden's profile, "Madonna Re-Creates Herself—Again," the *New York Times*, March 19, 1989, section 2, page 1.

103. *"It sharply rejects"*: Mark Hulsether, "Madonna and Jesus," *Christianity in Crisis*, July 15, 1991, 235–236.

104. *"I think what's important"*: *In Her Own Words*, 120.

105. *"more popular than Jesus now"*: Lennon quoted in *Shout! The Beatles in their Generation* (New York: Touchstone, 1981), 265.

105. *"the biggest disappointment"*: *In Her Own Words*, 113.

106. *"I may not be"*: *In Her Own Words*, 117.

CHAPTER SIX: IT'S A WONDERFUL DEATH:
THE CASE OF (MARTIN SCORSESE'S) JESUS CHRIST

109. *"To a filmwise viewer"*: The review is reprinted in its entirety (along with all Scorsese's movies through *Casino*) in Andy Dougan, *Martin Scorsese Close Up: The Making of his Movies* (New York: Thunder's Mouth Press, 1997), 129–130.

110. *"Capracorn"*: For a discussion of some of the objections to *It's a Wonderful Life*, see Raymond Carney, *American Vision: The Films of Frank Capra* (New York: Cambridge University Press, 1986), 379–380.

111. *Film historian Robert Ray*: Robert Ray, *A Certain Tendency of the Hollywood Cinema, 1930–1980* (Princeton: Princeton University Press, 1985), 213–215.

112. *evangelical ire*: For criticism of the movie and an explanation about why some of it was misplaced, see Carol Iannone, "The Last Tempation Reconsidered," published in the conservative Christian magazine *First Things* in February 1996 (50–54). I downloaded the piece from the journal's website: www.firstthings.com/ftissues/ft9602/ionnone.html. For an account of the controversy from the point of view of its critics, see Larry Poland and Robert Holmes, *The Last Temptation of Hollywood* (Mastermedia International, 1988). See also the appendix of *Scorsese on Scorsese*, a collection of the director's comments on his films edited by David Thompson and Ian Christie (1989; London: Faber and Faber, 1996).

113. *"I made it as a prayer"*: Scorsese quoted in Andy Dougan's introduction to *Martin Scorsese: A Journey*, edited by Mary Pat Kelly (1991; New York: Thunder's Mouth Press, 1996), 6. Along with Thompson and Christie's *Scorsese on Scorsese*, Kelly's book, a collection of interviews with Scorsese and many of his collaborators, are the best sources of sustained commentary of his work. Another useful book is Peter Brunette's *Martin Scorsese: Interviews* (Jackson, MI: University of Mississippi Press, 1999), which anthologizes twenty major newspaper and magazine pieces in which the director discusses his work. As this book was being written, another profile, "The Man Who Forgets Nothing," by Mark Singer, was published in the March 27, 2000, issue of the *New Yorker* (90–103). But some of the best sources of Scorsese commentary are not necessarily in print media. See, for example, the documentary he made for the 1995 British Film Institute, *A Century of Cinema: A Personal Journey with Martin Scorsese Through American Movies* (a companion book was published by Hyperion in New York in 1997). Finally, the DVD edition of *The Last Temptation of Christ*, released in 2000 by Universal, includes running commentary by Scorsese and others as the film plays, an invaluable research tool.

Much of this commentary is overlapping, as Scorsese repeats many of the same ideas, sometimes verbatim, in a variety of contexts. But taken together, it represents an unusually rich body of material for scholars, students, and film buffs.

113. *"a devout Catholic"*: Kelly, 242.

114. *exaggerated, even mythologized:* A good example of this is Scorsese's oft–cited seminary training. Lloyd Baugh, a Jesuit, notes that since Scorsese didn't get any farther than a year in a junior seminary, his theological training was little more than (Catholic) high school level. See Baugh's respectful, but largely critical, analysis of Scorsese's theological vision in *The Last Temptation of Christ* in his book *Imaging the Divine: Jesus and Christ–Figures in Film* (Franklin, WI: Sheed & Ward, 1997), 57–58. One suspects there may be similar hyperbole in the widespread gangsterism that sometimes surrounds descriptions of Scorsese's childhood.

114. *"We didn't care":* Scorsese quoted in Dougan, *Martin Scorsese Close Up*, 12.

114. *They were "Italian Italian":* Richard Corliss, ". . . And Blood," *Film Comment* September–October 1988, included in Brunette, *Interviews*, 114.

115. *"The first images I recall": Scorsese on Scorsese,* 118.

115. *"My friends used to say":* Guy Flatley, "He Has Often Walked Mean Streets," the *New York Times*, December 16, 1973, in Brunette, *Interviews*, 5 (emphasis in original).

115. *"For me, Holy Week":* Kelly, 29.

115. *"I thought a lot":* Scorsese quoted in Dougan, *Martin Scorsese Close Up*, 18.

116. *"To take a religion":* Scorsese quoted in Dougan, *Martin Scorsese Close Up*, 18; Kelly, 31.

116. *"I always wanted": Scorsese on Scorsese,* 117.

117. "Mean Streets *dealt: Scorsese on Scorsese,* 47.

118. *"Charlie uses other people":* Scorsese quoted in Dougan, *Martin Scorsese Close Up*, 38

118. *"Marty Scorsese was very intelligent":* Kelly, 32.

120. *"I realized":* Kelly, 227.

120. *The Last Temptation:* Information on Kazantzakis is gleaned from the brief biographical portrait by translator P. A. Bien (who has written widely about him) included at the end of *The Last Temptation of Christ* (1960; New York: Scribner's, 1998) and the remarks of his widow Eleni and others included in Kelly, 163–167.

121. *prolonged identity crisis:* The term is Iannone's. See *"The Last Temptation* Reconsidered."

121. *"When critics":* Schrader made these remarks in the third "chapter" of commentary included in the DVD edition of *The Last Temptation of Christ,* released in 2000.

121. *"He was not primarily interested": The Last Temptation of Christ,* 505.

122. *"My feeling"*: Scorsese on Scorsese, 215.

126. *"a fair objection"*: These and subsequent comments by Schrader come from the final "chapter" of the DVD for *Temptation*.

127. *"it came right out"*: Scorsese on Scorsese, 126.

127. *"When a lion appears"*: Janet Maslin's review, which appeared in the August 12, 1988 edition of the *Times*, is included in *The New York Times Guide to the 1,000 Best Movies Ever Made*, edited by Maslin and Vincent Canby (New York: Times Books, 1999), 471–473.

127. *"the essential Greekness"*: The Last Temptation of Christ, 502.

127. *"I was thinking"*: Scorsese on Scorsese, 127.

128. *"Anyone in authority"*: Corliss, "And Blood," in Brunette, *Interviews*, 116.

128. *"a faithful little negro"*: The Last Temptation of Christ, 451.

128. *Mary Magdalene first sees the resurrected Jesus*: John 20: 1–18.

128. *"for us one moment"*: The Last Temptation of Christ, 353.

128. *"I just couldn't see him"*: Kelly, 224.

129. *despite some misgivings*: "One problem I have in the book is the relationship between Jesus and Mary Magdalene," Scorsese said. "If there had to be a sexual temptation, it could have been another woman; for it to be Mary seemed kind of obvious." See *Scorsese on Scorsese*, 143.

129. *"Who are my mother and [my] brothers?"*: Mark 3: 31–35. *New American Bible* (Washington, D.C.: Confraternity of Christian Doctrine, 1986) included in *The Catholic Study Bible* (New York: Oxford University Press, 1990).

129. *"Marty told me"*: Kelly, 213.

129. *reception of* Last Temptation: Much of the following information comes from the appendix on the controversy in *Scorsese on Scorsese*, 211–217.

130. *The same five actors*: See, for example, the nineteenth "chapter" of commentary on the DVD for the movie.

130. *"With* Last Temptation*"*: Gavin Smith, "The Art of Vision: Martin Scorsese's *Kundun*," *Film Comment*, January–February 1998, in Brunette, *Interviews*, 248.

131. *"nothing to say about the Resurrection"*: See, for example, Dougan, *Martin Scorsese Close Up*, 53. Scorsese himself cites Principe on the DVD commentary for the film and elsewhere.

131. *"People would ask Willem"*: Kelly, 220.

Conclusion: The Souls of Kings

137. *"I should like"*: Martin Luther King, Jr., "The American Dream" in *A Testament of Hope: The Essential Writings and Speeches of Martin Luther King, Jr.*, edited by James M. Washington (San Franciso: HarperSanFrancisco, 1986), 208.

137. *"will one day live"*: Martin Luther King, Jr., "I Have a Dream," in *A Testament of Hope*, 219.

138. *"are taking our whole nation back"*: King, "The Time for Freedom Has Come," in *Testament*, 165 (for a variation of this remark, see "I See the Promised Land," also in *Testament*, 286); King, "I Have A Dream," in *Testament*, 219.

139. *"Longevity has its place"*: King, "I've seen the Promised Land," in *Testament*, 286.

140. *"militant secularists"*: For this phrase and Lasch's description of himself as an atheist, see Casey Blake and Christopher Phelps, "History as Social Criticism: Conversations with Christopher Lasch," *The Journal of American History* 80:4 (March 1994), 1313. It's important to note that in this extended interview, Lasch is talking about his youth. Neither here nor in his last two books does Lasch speak directly about his religious stance toward the end of his life. But essays such as "The Soul of Man Under Secularism," which look skeptically at the what he has dubbed a secular "therapeutic" culture, and his profound respect for figures like Martin Luther King—who he specifically celebrates for his avowedly religious orientation—make it hard to believe that he was wholly devoid of some kind of spiritual orientation. On his critique of secularism, see in particular the last two essays in his posthumous collection *The Revolt of the Elites and the Betrayal of Democracy* (New York: Norton, 1995); on King, see *The True and Only Heaven: Progress and Its Critics* (New York: Norton, 1991), 386–398 ff.

140. *"Hope implies a deep-seated trust"*: Lasch, *The True and Only Heaven*, 81.

INDEX

A

Abraham, 125
"Absolution," 55
Act Concerning Religion, 37
"Act of Contrition," 98, 99
Adam, James Truslow, 4
Adams, John, 17, 38
affirmative action, 138
African American culture, 103
African Americans, xv, 62, 70
After Hours, 123
Age of Innocence, The, 119
agnostics, 139
albums, 92, 98
Alexander VI, Pope, 18
Alger, Horatio, 8
Alice Doesn't Live Here Anymore,
    118
Alvin Ailey dance troupe, 90–91
American Revolution, 31
America, the name, 18
American Catholic Experience, The,
    xxiii
American Catholicism, 62, 141
American imagination, the, 102, 133
American Moses, 139
Americanism, 45–46
Anabaptists, 26
Antin, Mary 7
Antinomians, 33
antisegregation, 138
Arminius, Jacobus, 27
atheists, 139

B

Bailey, George, 109–112, 131–132
Bailey, Harry, 111, 131
Bailey, Mary, 110, 132
Baptists, 5
Barron, Joseph, 48
Barrymore, Lionel, 111
Beatles, the, 92, 98, 105
Beatty, Warren, 105

beauty, 96–97
Bedtime Stories, 105
"Benediction," 49
Benitez, (Jellybean) John, 91
Bergson, Henri, 120
Bible, the, 30
Bien, P. A., 121, 127
"big rock candy mountain," 12
Birth of a Nation, 70
black males (scapegoating of), 103
Black Reconstruction, 71
Black Sox Scandal, 53, 54
Bloom, Verna, 129
"Borderline," 94
Bowie, David, 125
Bradford, William, 22
Bradstreet, Anne, 26, 30
Bray, Stephen, 91, 99
Breen, Joseph, 66
Brucolli, Matthew, 50
Butler, Rhett, 65, 76–83

C

California Gold Rush, 12
Calvert family, the, 36–37
Calvert, Cecilius, 37
Calvert, George, 37
Calvin, John, 26–27, 126
Calvinist, 27, 29
Cana, 126
Cape Fear, 123
Cappa, Charlie, xxii, 117–118, 119
Capra, Frank, xxii, 2, 110, 111, 113,
    132
"Capracorn," 110
Carnegie, Andrew, 97
Carraway, Nick, 53–54, 58–61
Carroll, John, 38–39
Casino, 119
Catholic achievement, xix
Catholic confidence, xix
Catholic denial, 83
Catholic identity, 46, 87
Catholic imagination, 42

Catholic laity, 46
Catholicism legitimated, 38
Caton, Juliette, 128
Certain Sacrifice, A, 91
Chalcedon, Council of, 121
Charles I, King, 37
choice, 107, 133
Christ's passion, 102, 133
Ciccone, Silvio, 88–89, 100
Cimarrons, the, 19–20
Civil Rights Movement, the, 6,
    137–138
Civil War, English, 28, 34, 37
Civil War, States, xxi, 41, 69–70,
    102
Clinton-Lewinsky scandal, 21
Cocks, James, 123
Cody, Dan, 52
collective consciousness, 126
collective obligation, 140
Color of Money, The, 123
Columbus, Christopher, 17–18
commitment to reform, 140
common sense, 5
compact disk, 98
"concept" album, 98–99
confidence, 100
Constitution, the, 138
conversion, 31
Coppola, Francis Ford, 117, 119
Cortés, Hernan, 18
covenant of grace, 28
Crack-Up, The, 61
Cromwell, Oliver, 34, 37
cross, the, 102, 103, 118, 125
Crouch, Andrae, 101
Crucible, The, 21
crucifix, 95, 118, 123

D

Dafoe, Willem, 108 (photo), 123, 133
Danova, Cesare, 117
Darcy, Monsignor, 49
Dark Side of the Moon, 98
"Day of Doom," 35
De Niro, Robert, 117, 119, 122
de Champlain, Samuel, 18

de Tocqueville, Alexis, 4, 39–40, 61
Declaration of Independence, the, 5,
    137, 138
Democracy in America, 4, 39–40, 61
Democracy, foundations of, 23
Democratic Party, 39
denial, 133, 140
DePalma, Brian, 61
Desperately Seeking Susan,
    84 (photo), 94
destiny, 27, 132–133
Dick Tracy, 104
disco craze, 92–93
discrimination, xix, 41
Doctrine of Works, 27
Dolan, Jay, xxiii
Donato, Rafael, 114
double consciousness, xiv, xv–xvii,
    xxiii, 46, 54, 61, 107, 136, 139
doubt, 100
Drake, Sir Francis, 19–20
Dream of Celebrity, 96–97, 105
Dred Scott Decision, the, 6
DuBois, W. E. B., xiv (photo), xv–xvi,
    71, 136
Dylan, Bob, 92, 117

E

Eagles, the, 98
Eckleburg, T. J., 59
education, 29–30
Edwards, Jonathan, 35
Eliot, T. S., 59
Epic of America, The, 4
Erotica, 105
European colonization, xix
"Everybody," 91
Evita, 105
"Express Yourself," 93, 99
E.T., 119
Evangelical Sisterhood, the, 122
evil, 128

F

Farrell, James T., xxiii
Fay, Cyril Sigourney Webster, 48, 49

Fay, Daisy, 52–53, 57–58
fear, 100–101
Federal Housing Authority (FHA), 10
feminism, 93–94, 99
feminist theology, 104
Ferdinand, King, 18
Fiedler, Leslie, 49–50
First Great Awakening, the, 35
Fitzgerald, (Sayre) Zelda, ii (photo), 48–50
Fitzgerald, Annie, 68
Fitzgerald, Phillip, 68
Fitzgerald, Scott F., ii (photo), xxi, xxiv, 44 (photo), 45–62, 66, 94, 106
Fitzgerald, Scottie, 48
Forbes, Steve, 6
Ford, John, xxiii
Forging Ahead, 8
Fortin, Madonna, 88
Foster, Jodie, 119
Frank Sinatra Sings for Only the Lonely, 98
Franklin, Aretha, 101
Franklin, Benjamin, 7, 35–36, 97
freedom, 96, 107, 138
Freedom, American Dream of, 5–7, 62, 134
Frith, Simon, 91
fun, 96
Fundamentalist Baptist Tabernacle, 129

G

Gable, Clark, 65
Gabriel, Peter, 125
Gandhi, Mohandas, 139
Gates, Bill, 7
Gatsby, Jay, xxi, 52–62, 96
Gatz, Jimmy (James), 52
Gethsemane, 127
Gettysburg Address, the, 137
GI Bill, the, 9
Gilroy, Dan, 91
Glorious Revolution, the, 37
God and the individual, 122

God's Controversy with New England, 35
Godfather, The, 117, 119
Gone with the Wind, xxi, 6, 64, 65–83, 108, 131
Good Life, American Dream of, 11–13, 96
Goodfellas, 119
Gower, Mr., 111
grace, 96
"great American novel, the," 51–52
Great Depression, the, 4
Great Famine, the, 39
Great Gatsby, The, ii, xxi, 51–57, 131
Greek Passion, The, 120
Greeley, Andrew, xx
Gregory, Andre, 128
Griffith, D. W., 70
guilt, 96, 133

H

Hatch, Mary, 132
Hawks, Howard, 61
Hawthorne, Nathaniel, 21
Healy, Patrick, xvi
Hemingway, Ernest, 61
Henry VIII, King, 15, 20
Henry, Clifford, 72
Hernandez, Patrick, 91
Hershey, Barbara, 122
Hill, Lauryn, 98
Hinckley, John, 119
hip-hop, 93
Hitler, 102
"Holiday," 91
Home Ownership, American Dream of, 8–11, 65
Homestead Act, the, 9
Hoover, Herbert, 70
hope, 140
Hotel California, 98
How to Succeed in Business Without Really Trying, 8
Howard, Sidney, 66
Hulsether, Mark, 103–104
Hume, Cardinal Basil, 129
Hutchinson, Anne, 33–34

I

Iconoclasts, the, 121
immigrant aid society, 39
In the Wee Small Hours, 98
individual and God, 122
individual conscience, 30, 107
indulgences, 27
infant baptism, 31
Inquisition, the, 102
instructed conscience, 29
intolerance, 129
Ireland, John, 45
Irish diaspora, 39
irony, 119
Isaac, 125
Isabella, Queen, 18
It's a Wonderful Life, xxi, 2 (photo), 3, 109–112, 133

J

Jackson, Michael, 101
James I, King, 11–12
Jefferson, Thomas, 8, 137
jeremiad, 35
Jesus, 88, 94, 103, 105, 113, 120–128, 133
Jim Crow laws, 70
John the Baptist, 124, 128
John, Gospel of, 128
Judas Iscariot, 123–124, 128, 129
"Justify My Love," 105

K

Kamins, Mark, 91
Kazantzakis, Nikos, 112, 113, 120–121, 125–126, 127, 128, 129
"Keep it Together," 99
Keitel, Harvey, 117, 127, 129
Kennedy, Frank, 80
Key, Francis Scott, 46
King, Martin Luther, Jr., 6, 136 (photo)–141
Know-Nothing Party, 41
Ku Klux Klan, 68, 69–71, 102, 103
Kundun, 118

L

labor union, 39, 45
Lambert, Mary 102
LaMotta, Jake, 119
Lang, Pearl, 90–91
Lasch, Christopher, 140
"Last Ordeal, The," 49
Last Supper, the, 125, 126, 128
Last Temptation of Christ, The, xxii, 108 (photo), 112–134
Latham, Harold, 74
Latinos, xv
Laud, William, 27, 34
Lauper, Cyndi, 92
Lazarus, 124
League of Their Own, A, 105
Leigh, Vivian, 65
Lennon, John, 105
Leo X, Pope, 15
Leo XIII, Pope, 45
Leonard, Patrick, 99
Leslie, Shane, 48
Levitt, Abraham, 9
Levitt, Alfred, 9
Levitt, William, 9
Levittown, 9
life as journey, 140
Like a Prayer (album), 84, 98–100, 106–107
"Like a Prayer" (song), 84, 98, 100–104, 105
"Like a Prayer" (video), 84, 98, 102–104, 106
Like a Virgin (album), 94, 106
"Like a Virgin" (song), 85, 94, 100
"Like a Virgin" (video), 94, 100
Lincoln, Abraham, 9, 102, 137, 138
Line of Demarcation, 18
Lion King, The, 101
Lopez, Jennifer, 105
Lourdes (Madonna's daughter), 105
"Love Song," 99
Lucas, George, 119
"Lucky Star," 94
Luther, Martin, 15

M

Madonna, (Ciccone) xxi, xxii, xxiv, 84–107, 132
Madonna, 91
Magdalene, Mary, 120, 122, 123, 124, 125, 128, 129
Mamet, David, 97
"Man in the Mirror," 101
Mark, Gospel of, 129
marriage (sanctity of), 99
Marsh, John, 73
Martha (and Mary), 125
Mary (and Martha), 125
Mary (Jesus' mother), 95, 128
Mary (Virgin), 129
Maslin, Janet, 127, 130
"Material Girl" (song), 94, 95, 102
"Material Girl" (video), 94, 95, 102
Mayflower Compact, 23, 30
McCarthy, Mary, xxiii
McQuillan, Molly, 47
McQuillan, Philip Francis, 47
McVeigh, Timothy, 6
Mean Streets, xxii, 117–118, 119, 122
Meet John Doe, 110
Mencken, H. L., 21
Mennonites, xvi
Mercator, Geradus, 18
Miller, Arthur, 21
Miller, Rudolph, 55–56
Miseducation of Lauryn Hill, The, 98
Mitchell, Eugene, 68–69
Mitchell, Isaac Green, 68
Mitchell, Margaret, xxi, xxii, xxiv, 64 (photo)–75, 83, 94, 106
Mitchell, May Belle, 69, 72
Mitchell, Russell Crawford, 68
Mitchell, Stephens, 69
"Model of Christian Charity, A," 23–25
Moore, Paul, 130
morality, 102
Morris, Charles, 46
Mr. Smith Goes to Washington, 110
MTV, 92–93, 94, 98
Murray, John Courtney, xx
Music, 106

N

New World, the, 17–20
Nicaea, First Council of, 121
Nicaea, Second Council of, 121
Nicene Creed, xx
Nietzche, Friedrich, 120, 126
Ninety-five Theses, 15
nonviolence, 139
nuns, 87–88

O

O'Hara (Robillard), Ellen, 71–72, 75–76, 78–80, 83
O'Hara, Careen, 71, 79
O'Hara, Gerald, 68, 71–72, 75, 78
O'Hara, John, 50
O'Hara, Scarlett, xxi, 62, 64, 65, 75–83, 96
obsessive personality, 119
Of Plymouth Plantation, 22
"Oh, Father," 98, 100
"Open Your Heart," 95
opportunity, 5, 138
optimism, 140
Ovitz, Michael, 123
Oxenham, John, 19–20

P

"Papa Don't Preach," 95
Papal Index, the, 120
papists, 25–26
Paul (Saul), 125
Penn, Sean, 94, 97
Pepsi, 87
Peron, Eva, 105
personal responsibility, 140
Peter, 126
piety, 14, 30, 33, 86, 99, 104
Pilgrims, 14, 22–23, 32
Pink Floyd, 98
Pius XI, Pope, 49
police violence, 103
Pontius Pilate, 125
Poor Richard's Almanac, 35
pop music, 93–94, 105

post-Kennedy generation, 106
postmodernism, 93–94
Potter, Henry, 111
power, 96
preparationism, 27–29, 33, 139
Presley, Elvis, 12, 92, 101
Prince, 99
Principe, Frank, 118, 121, 130
"promise of American life, the," 42
"Promise to Try," 98, 100
Promised Land, The, 7
"Protestant" model, 38
Protestant Ethic and the Spirit of Capitalism, The, 24
Protestant imagination, the, 139
Puritans (Puritanism), 5–6, 21–42, 121, 132, 134, 139
Pyron, Darden Asbury, 67

Q

Quebec Act, 38
Quinn, Aidan, 122, 123

R

race, 101–103
rage, 119
Raging Bull, 119
Raleigh, Sir Walter, 20
Ray of Light, 104, 106
Ray, Robert, 111–112
Reagan, Ronald, 25, 93, 119
Reed, Donna, 110, 132
Reformation, the, xix, 14–15, 27
Reformist impulse, 15
Reservoir Dogs, 85, 104
"Respect," 101
resurrection, 125, 126, 131
Ritchie, Guy, 106
Robbins, Anthony, 8
Robe, The, 116
Robinson, Amy, 117
rock and roll, 92–93
Rolling Stones, the, 99
Romani, 45
Root of the American Dream, 13–15
Rossellini, Roberto, 116

Rothstein, Arnold, 54

S

Sarnemington, Blatchford, 56
Satan, 125, 128
Saul (Paul), 125
Scarface, 61
schools, parochial, 45–46, 89
schools, public, 45
Schrader, Paul, 113, 121, 122, 123, 125, 126
Schwartz, Adolphus, 55, 56
Scorsese, Catherine, 114
Scorsese, Charles, 114
Scorsese, Martin, xxii, xxiv, 108 (photo), 112–134
"Secret," 105
segregation, 102
Selnick, David O., 66
Separatists, 22–23, 28, 32
Sex, 105
sex, 93, 106
Sgt. Pepper's Lonely Hearts Club Band, 98
sin, 96
Sinatra, Frank, 83, 92, 98
"Sinners in the Hands of an Angry God," 35
slavery, 62, 102
Sly and the Family Stone, 99
Smith, Al, 41, 70
Smith, Captain John, 12
social justice, 139
songs (individual), 93
Souls of Black Folk, The, xiv, xv
South, the, 6, 70
"Spanish Eyes," 100
Spears, Britney, 105
Speed the Plow, 97
Spice Girls, the, 105
Spielberg, Steven, 119
Springsteen, Bruce, xviii, 93
Staple Singers, the, 99
Star Wars, 119
Stegner, Wallace, 12
Stephens, John, 68
Stephens, Mary Isabelle, 68–69

Stewart, Jimmy, 3, 109, 110, 111
Sticky Fingers, 99
Strive and Succeed, 8
Struggling Upward, 8
Surratt, Mary, 46
surrender, 133
Sweet, Deborah Margaret, 68

T

"Take a Bow," 105
Tara, 65, 79
Tarantino, Quentin, 85
Taxi Driver, 119
Temple, the, 125, 126
Tender Is the Night, 50, 55
Tenth Muse, The, 26
Testem Benevolentiae, 45–46
This Side of Paradise, 49
"Till Death Do Us Part," 98, 99
transubstantiation, 126
Treaty of Tordesillas, 18
True and Only Heaven, The, 140
True Blue, 94
Truth or Dare, 86, 95, 105

U

uncertainty, 100
Upshaw, Berrien (Red), 73–74
Upward Mobility, American
    Dream of, 7–8

V

vanity, 104
Vatican II, xvii, 19
Vatican, the, xix, 45, 86
Vespucci, Amerigo, 18
Veterans Authority (VA), 10
violence, 119
Virginia Company, the, 11–12

W

Waldseemüller, Martin, 18
Warhol, Andy, 99
Warner Brothers, 91

Washington, George, 12, 17
"Waste Land, The," 59
Watson, Tom, 69
wealth, 96
Weber, Max, 24
West, the, 12
Wigglesworth, Michael, 35
Wildmon, Donald, 85
Wilkes, Ashley, 72, 75–77, 81–82
Wilkes, Melanie, 72, 75–76, 78–79,
    81–83
Williams, Roger, 32
Wilson, Edmund, 48
Wilson, George, 59
Winfrey, Oprah, 86
Winthrop, John, 16 (photo), 23–24,
    32
Wolfe, Thomas, 9
Wolfsheim, Meyer, 54
World War II, 9
Wasserman, Lou, 112
Wayne, John, 116
Wharton, Edith, 119
women, 128
Wainwright, Sam, 132

Y

youth (cult), 97

Z

Zorba the Greek, 112